My Father's Young Life: A Memoir

MY FATHER'S YOUNG LIFE: A MEMOIR

The father I never knew...

Jean Caroline

ISBN-13:978-1500625009
ISBN-10:1500625000

Polish Born: Stanislaus Przybzla, Fall River, Massachusetts
Nov. 10, 1909 - Jan. 15, 1992

Stanislaus is Polish for Stanley; however, he changed his last name after
he married, to Stanley Priscilla, the difficulty others had with Przybzla was the
reason he gave.

DEDICATION
I dedicated this work to and in memory
of my father and mother and their lives
in the early Twentieth Century.

INTRODUCTION
Following this page you will find a letter my father sent me, which was included with his writings. His letter expressed his thoughts and feelings concerning why he felt he needed to write his story, as he put it, to help explain the reasons for what mistakes he felt he made in being a father. In editing, I tried to keep his writings as close to his thought as possible.

As I worked on compiling, writing and editing his notes, I learned so much about who he was within himself, the person so different from the man I knew as dad, that if this were wholly my own work I would have titled it: THE FATHER I NEVER KNEW, for I realized we hardly ever really know our parents and learning who he was within himself, I love him more.

ACKNOWLEDGEMENT
I give a very special *'thank you,'* to my son Paul Westerman Jr., for his interest, help and encouragement.

Dear Little One,

For quite a while, I have been thinking of writing something about my young life. One reason is to share with you my life as I remember it. The second reason and perhaps the most important; is that maybe after reading my story you will find a clue, if there is one, to better understand why I did things that may have hurt you as you were growing up at home and if you do then maybe you will forgive.

My own growing up was not easy, I knew what it was to go hungry and have nothing. We as a family lived "without" all my young life. Now as I spend my last years and look back I see I was not the father I should have been, my goal was providing for my family, I spent too much of my time working, hoping to provide well so my family wouldn't have to go without as we did when I was growing up. When your mother and I married we began to have a family quite soon and working hard was what I felt was the right thing for me to do.

I hope you will not judge me harshly for the wrongs I may have done or how I may have displeased you. Perhaps understanding my life might help you understand me better. I am not trying to find a loophole, or crying on anyone's shoulder, what you read in these notes is the truth, but one thing I want to stress is, I do not want you to think ill of my parents; I love them and always have. Yes, my life could have been better if they were different but I sincerely believe they did the very best they knew how to do. I know that my father wanted to say he was sorry before he died but somehow he could not bring himself to do so, at least I had that feeling.

I send this to you Jeannie because I know you like to write and maybe someday you will do something with it. You will have a very big job ahead of you for you will find mistakes, words missing and misspelled and an enormous job of piecing it all together but I know you can do it. Please excuse me and please do not misplace these notes. When you have created a readable book I would like to have your sister and brother know my story too; this way they also will know me better and maybe understand why I did the things I did.

Your Dad, I love you.

CONTENTS

CIRCA 1909 – 1925
Childhood Years

Before I start about myself, I will say a few words about my mother and father, things I learned from their conversations, which I overheard while growing up and remember still. My father was born in a place that was at that time known as Galicia, and was under the Russian rule. I remember when mom and dad would have a little argument she would always call him a Russian, but I think that was only to tease him, because he was a Pole. My understanding is that he was an orphan and he had a half-brother who married my mother's sister. In addition, my father was an army man in his own country. How long he served, I don't know. He was a big man a little over six feet, and a big chest; I will write more about him later.

Now a little about my mother, she was born in Poland. Her folks had a farm and a butcher shop. I never learned much about her mother, but her father was a big man, she always said that I took after him. She had sisters and brothers, how many I do not know however, she was the elder of her siblings. She and her father made a few trips from Poland to America, for what reason I also don't know but on their last trip to America, my mother stayed, and her father went back. Later one of her sisters came to America; she is the sister who married my father's half-brother. My mother never saw any of the rest of her family even though another sister had come from Poland to live in Canada. It is sad to think about mom never being able to see her sister because we were all a very poor family and didn't have money for such things as travel. Yes, we were poor but one thing I can say for sure, we all had enough to eat

As I progress making notes, you will learn more about my parents but for now, I will begin my own young history I will begin back as far as I can remember. The first thing that comes to mind is a street called Slade Street. In front, there was a butcher and grocery store; behind the store, there were two houses. We lived in the second house; each house had four families living in it, our apartment was upstairs. I remember sitting by the window many times and looking at the hearse that was in the next yard. I remember that while I was looking at it, I was not thinking of it as a death wagon but rather from the standpoint of how it was built. The carving, the purple drapes, the rims of the wheels were rubber, and the back wheels were larger than the front ones. The driver had nothing to protect him from getting wet in case of rain. I guess, maybe someone would hold an umbrella over him while traveling in the funeral. Now that is one of the things I remember looking at; another was watching men kill a rat that was caught in a cage. In those days, we had rats, and whenever anyone would trap a rat, all the men in both houses would then try to kill it. Nine out of ten chances they would. All the kids in those houses would have to stay home until the ordeal was over. However, all of us would have our noses pressed to the windows to watch. I guess many of us kids felt sorry for the poor thing because it didn't have much of a chance to get away, and killing it, had to be done.

In our apartment, the floors were all wood; no wall-to-wall carpets in those days just a few throw rugs. I remember my mom scrubbing the floor every Friday because Saturday was a big day for us kids. You see the man that owned those houses came around every Saturday to collect the rent so mom would clean the house and dress us up nice because he would give each of us two or three cents to spend for candy. That was a happy time for us and we looked forward to each Saturday. He was a small man, all gray hair but always nicely dressed. He would always make a nice comment to mom about how nice the house looked that would please her very much. I remember how she would scrub the floor but she could never get it as clean as her neighbor's floors and they would never tell her why. When I grew much older, I realized they were using bleach, that's what made their floors so clean and my mom wanted her floors like theirs, when I think of it now I feel sorry for her. Another thing that happened on that day was my mother's sister would come over and she would bring candy. My sister Rose was her pet and she would give her some and not us. That is all she had to do and we, my brother Walter and other sister Jean would start crying. My father would get angry and holler at her and then we would get some candy too. She was teasing us and having a little fun in her own way. She was the sister who married my father's half-brother. Now that I think of it, I very seldom saw her husband with her at our house, maybe my father and he didn't get along I don't know but it is odd after all these years I should think of that.

Well back to my story, we must have lived in that house for quite a spell because my mother had two sets of twins while we lived there but I only remember one set. I remember seeing her holding them on her lap and I knew they were ill because I heard my mom talking about them. I will tell you a little story about this incident concerning a woman who lived close by. As I said before, remembering those twins on my mothers' lap, I also remember this woman came to the house; she looked in one of the twin's mouth and put her finger in to push down the tongue to see the throat but what was said I do not know. Not long after, the twins died. My mother always said that the woman was the cause of the twins dying. She would say many times after, that the woman was a witch. She did have some funny habits but I do not think she was a witch. I remember the twins passing away but I remember nothing of the funeral. I just remember seeing them on her lap.

Next, I remember we were living in another house on Peckham Street. There were a few houses grouped together on a large lot and our house was next to a stable which rented out wagons and horses to people who went around buying junk from house to house; the stable also rented to fruit peddlers. We kids would play around the horses, crawling under them and none of us ever got hurt. I guess because they were old horses and too lazy to move. In that house two things happened that I remember well. Not many homes had electric lights those days, and the one we lived in had no electric lights or gaslights, all the light we had was what we could get from a kerosene lamp. Well this one evening mom had to put kerosene in the lamp, dad would usually do this but he was working nights then. We kept the kerosene under the sink and when mom went to fill the lamp, she spilled some on the floor. Not thinking, I heard her say, "I'll light a match to it and let it burn out." In a second, the room was on fire. The fire department came, they put out the fire and we kids had to sleep at the neighbors. Let me make it clear, it was an honest mistake on my mothers' part because she was a smart, hard working mom. In that same house, I had the misfortune of getting sick, with scarlet fever. I remember mom washing my sheets every day, for how long I do not know but it must have been quite a while.

When I got a little better, I wanted to go out and play, mom didn't want me to go because she knew that I was very weak. Finally, after pestering her day after day she gave in. I remember this as if it was yesterday, I was weak and I had to hold on to the windowsills of the stores because the wind had control over me. Yet, do you think being in that condition, I would go in the house? No, not me, I loved the outside, I loved to play and even if not playing I wanted to stay outdoors. The sickness kept me out of school for some time; I must have been in my third year of school. When I was ready to return to school, I was so happy. I wanted to get there early because I knew what I was going to do. This may sound foolish now but at the time, to me, it meant everything. When I got there, I kissed the schoolhouse, not because I loved to learn but because I was healthy and alive and enjoyed the out-of–doors so much. I really cannot express the feelings I had at that time; I just remember I had tears in my eyes while kissing the schoolhouse. I was so happy and I can still remember that happiness as if it were yesterday. I will mention here that up to this time I didn't know my father very well, I don't remember seeing him much I suppose because he was working nights and slept in the daytime and we were at school.

The next thing I recall is living in a different house. This house was on East Main Street, which was one of the main streets in our town. I guess I never mentioned we lived in Fall River, Massachusetts. We had an apartment in this house and it must have been over a store because we had to climb about fifteen steps to get to it from the back of the house. There was a small yard with a high fence in the back. Behind the fence was an alley but it also served as a street because there were many houses facing it. I remember a beer wagon would come by selling beer. One time my dad told me to buy two bottles and as the man handed them to me over the fence one bottle dropped on my nose and ever since then I have had trouble breathing through that side, I guess something was broken inside and never mended properly, and you know it still makes me angry at times.

Strange how something like that can happen so long ago and bother you all your life.

Now I am going to tell you something that I had the opportunity to see. What kids will do sometimes. There were two brothers living in the next house, we played in the same yard. I cannot remember how the conversation started but it came down to this. The older brother said,

"I can make my brother do anything I tell him to do."

I guess I said, "Let's see."

Then he took a can, pissed into it and told his younger brother to drink it, and sure enough, he did. I remember looking somewhat surprised at the two of them but I can never forget it. Sometimes I think of that incident and wonder what was going on in the mind of the older boy. I guess the younger one didn't know any better.

I don't remember how long we lived there but our next house was on the same street. It was in this house that I spent most of my life. Let me clarify this a little. In my mind, I did more, and experienced more of my young life there. This house was a four family house with three stores underneath, one was a Chinese laundry, another a tailor shop, and the third a shoe repair shop. I used to work in the Chinese laundry once a week washing shirts using a scrub brush on the collars. The owner, if I recall correctly, paid me fifty-cents for three or four hours of work, in those days that was quite a bit for a child to earn. He was a very nice old man and I learned a few words in Chinese but only remember a couple now. The man who ran the shoe repair shop was French; he had a peg leg of wood that is all I remember of him. The man who ran the Tailor shop was short and fat; he would send me to the store if he ran low on something and that way I earned a dime. I would always make sure he seen me looking in the shop window, that way if he needed anything he would send me. I think I made a pest of myself sometime by looking in the window too often. However, he never said anything to me about it, I am sure he knew I just wanted to earn a dime and he could not blame me for trying.

Now a little about the people that lived in this house. We lived on the top floor and across from us lived a French family with six children. I used to play with the boys, they were my age, one boy was named Sammy the other Willy, their father was a hard worker, and I remember the mother had men in the house when he was at work. I know this because sometimes he would return home early and catch a man there then there would be a loud and long argument, this happened quite a few times. Under us lived a Polish family, the father was working in the Tailor shop, and he was a chain smoker, I never seen him without a cigarette in his mouth. In the mornings, we could hear him coughing for at least ten minutes. He died after a couple years. They had five children, three boys and two girls. I remember one of the girls was born with the skin on her body like fish scales, if she would hurt or bump herself she would bleed a lot, and at that time, I guess there was no help for her. She never went out with any boys and one day she and a few other girls went to New Jersey to become nuns but she was rejected and not long after, she committed suicide. In addition, one of her brothers fell off a high building in New York while washing windows; I don't have to tell you what happen to him. I have gotten ahead of myself somewhat, let me back up. After the father died not long after the mother died also, leaving the sick girl, being the oldest, to become head of the family that was until she decided to try to become a nun. I guess she had nothing to look forward to in the outside world and failing at becoming a nun, she became so depressed she killed herself.

Next door to them lived another Frenchman and his wife, not a young couple, perhaps in their late fifty's. His wife chewed tobacco and drank quite a bit. Sometimes he would stop me in the hallway and talk to me, and although I was young, I guess he must have been lonely. He would say to me, "My wife won't live too long and then I will enjoy life. However, one Saturday he went out to get a haircut, it was a foggy, nasty day and he was hit and killed by a truck, so he never did get to enjoy his life the way he wanted. I always remembered what he said about his wife dying like he wished she would die. It taught me never to wish for anyone's death because what you wish upon someone else could happen to you instead.

Now to tell you a little about our apartment, coming in through the back door, we hardly ever used the front door, I don't know why we just never did. As you came through the back door, looking straight ahead you looked into the pantry, it was a good-sized pantry, next to it was my bedroom, next to my bedroom was my sister's room and next to her room was my parent's room. The kitchen was quite large and containing a coal stove and a very big table. We spent ninety-five percent of our time in the kitchen. Off the kitchen was the bathroom, there were two panes of glass in the door, why the glass who knows. Actually, there were two bathrooms side-by-side one for us and one for the people who lived next door.

The wall between the bathrooms didn't go all the way to the ceiling and the neighbors had a small boy; his name was Giga that is what they called him. He was a red head and whenever I went to the bathroom and he would be in their bathroom I would get a little water in a can and spill it on his head. Then he would holler "Ma! Ponana" throw water on me." His mother seemed not aware that the wall did not reach the ceiling so she would tell him to shut-up. Now to explain the word Ponana, in our town the majority of the people were French Canadians and anytime they got angry with us or any polish person they called us Polander, this little boy could not pronounce the word correctly, so therefore the word Ponana. Now back to explaining the rest of the apartment. The Kitchen was next to our parlor, now a day called the living room; next to that room was another bedroom, which was used only in the summer because the one wood/coal stove in the kitchen could not warm up the entire apartment so during the winter the parlor and that bedroom were closed off.

In this house, I began to know my father better because he was then working days. When he would come home from work one of us kids would take off his shoes, that was done every day, I guess that was the way it was done in Europe and followed here as a sort of tradition. On Saturday night, it was my job to shine my father and mothers shoes for next day Sunday mass. I seem only to remember my sisters Jean, Rose and Veronica; Veronica was beautiful; with long blond hair, she was very dainty as I recall. Sadly, she passed away, I remember the last breath she took as though it were yesterday. However, before I go into that there is a little story about her. A block or so from us was a little grocery store, operated by a Jewish family, and they wanted to adopt my little sister Veronica, they even wanted to pay mom some money if she only would let them have her. Naturally, mom would not think of such a thing. Quite a while after that Veronica became sick, possibly a cold at first then she ran a fever, mom and dad were both working at the time, my sister Rose was to mind her and keep her in the house. She had orders not to go outside but Rose's girlfriend came over and probably talked her into going out for a walk. What Rose did was wrap little Veronica in a blanket and put her into the carriage then Rose and her friend walked up and down the sidewalk. When my father arrived home from work and saw little Veronica in the carriage he really became angry, and he always seemed to blame Rose for Veronica's death because right after being outside with Rose, Veronica developed a high fever a very sore throat and I think it turned into Diphtheria. I rather blame my folks also because they should have called the doctor however; in those days, you didn't call the doctor as you do today. Well as I remember she became very bad one day; the rooms were hot because we had the stove burning, but the parlor was cooler so mom thought she would put Veronica in there, when mom picked her up to move her, Veronica died in our mother's arms, I still can remember it so clearly. When she was laid out in her pretty coffin, which was white and when no one was around I leaned over and kissed her on the cheek. I still remember how she looked in her days of life and in her coffin, I am sure she is an angel in heaven. So far, that made five deaths in our home, two sets of twins and Veronica, Mother had one more child but she really suffered giving birth that last time. You could hear her screaming a block away and the baby died at birth that was six deaths. I hardly remember when Elizabeth, Agnes and Henry were born so I should get back to my life story.

I was a very active child. I could not sit still, I always wanted to play and the day was always too short for me. If I ran out of playmates I would do something by myself. I would go to the dumping ground to look for things; I was always on the lookout for clocks, because my father's hobby was fixing clocks. If I found one or anything else, he would like I would hide it so that if anything happen, like if I stayed out too late and thought I would get heck I would bring the clock or whatever to him and that would keep my father from getting angry. Sometimes this saved me from getting a beating. I was frightened of my father, because he thought by putting fear in a child that was the way to bring him up. Oh, how wrong he was. Before my sister Veronica died, he had started to work days one week and then the next week he would work nights. So when four o'clock would roll around and dad would turn the corner and be out of sight it seemed the world was my own, it was a relief, I was free to play because mom was not that strict. I could not understand my father, maybe because he could never get ahead money wise. I am sure they had problems trying to raise a family those days and with having six children to bury, that must have been heart breaking alone. However I want to tell you now that I did not resent my father then nor do I resent him now, he thought he was doing right, he did the very best he could. Now back to my story.

My mother showed me a little more loving in my young years. I felt sorry for mom she was a hard working mother and Dad did very little to help raise us, or around the house for that matter. We children had our duties to perform each day, whether to bring coal up from the cellar, chop some wood to start the fire in case it went out during the night, bring the throw rugs outside hang them on the cloths line and beat them with carpet beaters to get the dirt and dust out. Besides my chores I was always trying to make a little money one way or another, I used to get up early take my bag and look through the trash barrel for rag, bottles, copper, lead, zinc, brass and once a week I would sell what I could to the junk man. I would give the money to mom and keep fifty cents or a dollar, it would depend on how much I made, but she would know how much I kept. On Saturdays, I would go to Jewish homes and light their fires for them because they could not do any sort of work on Saturdays, their Sabbath, a rule of their religion. Another thing I would do is look for deposit bottles and turn them in for a few cents, I would do anything to make spending money, because we only were given two or three cents a week from our parents, and that didn't go very far. The only toy I ever received from my mom and dad was a three-wheeler bicycle that they purchased with stamps they were saving. Any other toys I ever had were found in the trash if broken I would wait until I found another then make one out of the two. When I grew older I wanted a two-wheeler, I guess every boy wants a two-wheeler, well to get one I had to scrimp and save but finally I had enough money to buy one it cost fifteen dollars but as luck would have it I didn't have it long. Once riding across a street I was hit by a car bent the bike out of whack. My mom and dad got eighty dollars from the insurance company, but the bike was never fixed. I think they had a guilty feeling about that because that bike was with them even after they moved from Fall River to New Jersey, and I was married to your mother, they had it hanging in their garage. One time they rather hinted to me that they were sorry they had not had the bike repaired, but I couldn't blame them, back at that time money was hard to come by. As a kid, I was sorry they had not had it fixed, but I did find another bike in Rhode Island. It was a three-mile walk and often my friends and I walked there, this one time

when we were there I saw a bike in the trash bin, it was all apart and it took me two trips to get all the parts home. One of the boys that was with me and saw me take it; here is the sorry part, after I had put it all together and it was a pretty good bike, I guess he became jealous so he told the police. The police came to our house and one of them took a ride on it in the yard and took it away. They had no case against me but they brought me to court and put me on six months' probation, I had to report every Saturday morning to them. After a while I quit going and heard nothing more from them and of course I lost my bike again. There was no justice in any of it; my father was aware of that fact, he had no money to fight it, even if he did, they would make it tough for him because the French ran the town and they were not fond of the Polish. Therefore, as for toys the only ones we ever had were if someone gave us one. My folks could not afford to buy them, so most of our enjoyment was playing with other children. I would make dollhouses for the girls, I call them dollhouses, but actually, they were just cardboard boxes with holes cut out for windows and a door.

While I am writing, I keep thinking about how we spent Christmas. I just cannot find the words to tell you how much I loved that holiday. Sometimes, when I think of the way I felt then I get tears in my eyes; not because of gifts, we never got anything much. I remember one Christmas I received a ten-cent book and a tin rake and shovel, they were about six inches long; I would lie on my bed face down with my head hanging over the side and make believe I was a farmer, and rake on the wooden floor. I read the book and was happy to receive it.

Before I go any further, I will say a few words about the way we observed our Christmas. Weeks before the holiday mom would make paper flowers, lots of them. Dad would make frames out of wire to fit the frames of the pictures of Saints that hung on our walls, when the flowers were complete, they were put around the frames dad made and put on the pictures. Dad would then hang a wire holder from the ceiling, in the holder he would put a glass filled with cooking oil, on top of the oil a wick was put to float, he would then light the wick and it would stay lit for days. The house would then be cleaned from top to bottom, I mean everything was cleaned, all the curtains the floors scrubbed we all helped. Mom would do all the cooking the day before Christmas, Christmas Eve; she would make many pastries and a seven-course dinner all of which were made of grains. Dad would go outside, get some hay and place it under the tablecloth in the center of the table, to formed a little mound, just in back of the mound he would place two candles and a cross. At dinner time the candles were lit and mom would serve the food one course at a time. She would then sit down and we would eat a little of that dish, and again she would get up take that dish away and bring another dish, we would eat a little of it and this went on until all seven dishes were served; it was always such a nice meal. After dinner, nothing had to be done or could be done, as the day was Christmas Eve the holiday of holidays and we could not touch a broom or do any work what so ever. I remember it was such a warm feeling; Christmas was the best time in my young life because at home it seemed that there was peace in every ones heart. The day represented Christ; I think that was why everyone was mellow and kind. The next day, Christmas Day we would get up and there the Christmas tree would be, all dressed up with apples, oranges a few candies, dad had put hay under the tree as he always did. There was of course lots of food from Christmas Eve's dinner. We all would go to morning service at church, and the church would be all-prettied up with flowers everywhere. The choir would sing Christmas songs and it just made one feel wonderful. Oh, I remember those days so well. We kids would lie under the tree with our heads on the hay, it would smell so nice under there, and so cozy we would fall asleep. In the evening dad would read to us from two old Polish books, they were both about six inches square and four inches thick. You see mom was unable to read so dad was elected. The stories were fun stories, mom would get a big thrill and enjoy them so

very much, it was a wonderful way to spend Christmas day; I will never forget those Christmas days. Oh! Before I go any further, I must tell two things that happen the day before Christmas. The store owner across the street from us would have a young man dress as Santa Claus, he would ride a sled, the horses would have bells on and every so often he would throw a hand full of new pennies and we kids would try to pick up as many as we could. There were always so many kids that sometimes I would only get three or four cents that is if I was lucky. The other thing that I forgot to mention was this; before we ate, the seven-course dinner mom would have some holy wafers she had gotten from the sisters 'Nuns". The kind you get at Holy Communion only much bigger, about five by seven inches, dad would break it into small pieces and starting with mom he would wish her luck, health and that some day after death we would see each other in heaven. Mom would then do the same to him and take a piece of his host. He would then start with us children, that continued until we wished each other the same thing, and then we would sit down and eat dinner. It was about a week later that we celebrated the coming of the Three Kings; dad would write their initials above the door, they were K, M, and B. My dad had very nice hand writing, very fancy letters and in Polish, Kasper, Mayher and Bartoli. On that day dad would put a half dollar in a pan of water and we would wash ourselves with it as best we could because it kept falling out of our hands. I never understood the reason we did this, I guess I should have asked, maybe for health, money I can't say I was only about thirteen years old then and some of these practices came from the old country, Poland.

Another fond memory is of the church picnics we attended each year, which were held for the first few years in an area where we had to cross a lake to get there; I enjoyed that very much; up until that time, I had never been on a boat. The picnic area was so nice, lots of trees and open fields with green grass and wild flowers, we kids had a wonderful time playing all sorts of games. Mom would always bring homemade sausage and home baked bread and after running around playing, the sausage and bread sure tasted good. Dad would get high on beer and the whiskey that they would bring with them, he never became drunk, just feeling good and then it would be hard to get him to go home, he would want to stay until the last moment and by that time, we would all be tired and want to go home. It was always that way with my dad on these picnics.

At the picnics, there would be raffles and mom would try to win a blanket but she never did and she would get downhearted about that. I remember before one picnic held at the church grounds; it had rained during the night and in the morning mom sent me out to get some day old cake at the bakery across the street. As I came out of the house everything was so clean after the rain even the air seemed to smell better, as I was stepping off the curb there in the water was a half dollar, it stood out so bright in the water, and that was a great deal of money to find in those days. I made the trip to the bakery came home but didn't tell anyone about the half dollar, I was probably thinking about all the ice cream cones I could buy at the picnic. Well when we arrived at the picnic, I went off to walk around by myself and I came to where they were selling chances on blankets and there was mom, I didn't know how many times she played but she had not won. I could see the disappointment again in her face, a priest came by and she was so frustrated by not winning she told him the spinning wheel was fixed. I stood there, I remember feeling very sad that she had said what she did because I knew it was not true, right then and there I knew what I was going to do with the money I had found. I bought five chances at ten cents apiece and believe me I said a little prayer; oh I hoped so much to win and surprise my mother. If there was a time that I needed luck in my young life I felt that was the time, but I didn't win and there went my ice cream cones; I really felt bad that God hadn't answered my prayer and let me win a blanket for my mother.

I find I am remembering so many things to note down about my young life; some are short stories, some long. I will do the best I can.

During school vacation mom and dad would be working, not both at the same place. One year, mom worked at a hat factory, they made felt hats for men. I would always bring her lunch and while there I would help her, while mom was eating I would pull some hats out of the big vats they were in, I think it was dye and very hot, mom had to do so many a day then she could go home. I would get them out on the table and they had to be stretched to a certain measurement. The hats were folded like a piece of pie, only the top was not pointed it was more rounded. Mom had a stick with a mark on it so the hats had to be pulled each way until it was on the mark, after working with the hat for a while my hands would be the color of nicotine, I helped every time I brought her lunch but as soon as lunch was over, I had to go home. She appreciated my help because she would always pat my head, give me a smile, which always made me feel good inside. I was a little closer to my mother than my father, I can't explain it fully, it seemed there was always something on my fathers' mind and you could not get close to him. However, don't get me wrong I loved my dad and I forgave him for everything that I thought was wrong he ever said or did to me. There is one thing I didn't do and I should have, of course it was years later after I was married to you mother. About a week before he passed away he went to the hospital, I gave him a shave and after I finished I wanted to kiss him but I didn't, I don't know why I didn't follow my intuition, I am sorry to this day that I didn't. Even though he never showed me any love, I loved him. He was the kind of man I guess, who could not help the way he was. In my young days I didn't know any different so I accepted it as it was, for me my main thoughts were, just as long as I can go out and play everything else didn't really matter. I remember once, in the winter, I wanted to go out to play but my dad had not fixed my shoes, so I put on my sister's shoes. They were black and white with buttons on the side. Snow was on the ground, and people would look at my shoes because they were summer shoes but I didn't care. If dad would not fix my shoes I would go to the cellar and fix them myself; I would do anything needed but please do not stop me from going out to play. This always playing and all the time on the go caused me a lot of misery and for my folks too, but more about that later.

Now I am fourteen years old out of school, looking for work, times were bad and there were not many jobs to be found. Mom tried to teach me how to weave cloth in the mill where she was working at that time; in those day the management would let you teach one of your family members, but you received no pay, I tried it out but I didn't like it at all. It was very noisy, all them looms going I hated it. A short time later I moved into the spinning room, I had twenty machines to take care of, by that I mean I had to keep them clean and sweep the floor many, many times a day. The pay was $8.50 a week, mom received eight dollars and I received fifty cents. Here is how I spent it, ten cents for a cigar, fifteen cents for malted milk and twenty-five cents to go to the movie Sunday night, and that went on week after week.

Now I am going to back up a bit and tell you the part that I don't like to remember and why I said earlier how my being so active caused my folks and me a lot of grief. All those years I was wetting the bed. I don't know why, God only knows how hard I tried not to, I would stay up as late as I could; then when dad told me to get to bed I would go to the bathroom and force myself to get every drop out but that didn't help. It got to the point that every morning I would get a beating from my dad with a rope. He was working nights, when he returned home at six o'clock in the morning he would pull the sheets off me and if the bed was wet, I got the rope. That really hurt on bare skin. It went on for weeks, I don't know why he thought that a beating every morning would cure me. I really could not blame them after so many years a person gets tired of the same thing. Many years later, I found out that too much activity

during the day sometimes causes one to become so tired and sleep so soundly that the urge to go to the bathroom could not wake them up. Well anyway, after working a few months I decided to go to New York with a friend. I told my folks and I kept a few weeks' pay, I had a feeling that they did not mind my leaving, because dad never said to stay and mom although she did, but it was not with a real desire for me to stay. Therefore, when the day came for me to go, mom put ten dollars in my vest pocket and sewed it up, I was not to touch it except in case of an emergency, and off I went.

When my friend and I arrived, in New York, we went to a Polish home, not a regular home it was really a hall, and any one new to the city could sleep there for three days free of charge. After three days we were both ready to return home. Not knowing where to look for work we started to go to the docks where the ships were tied and asking if there was work, we could do aboard the ships. One day on our way to the docks we saw a sign in a window of a shop, "Boy Wanted", we walked in and I got the job. The job was filling small bottles with baby oil and small containers with baby powder. I started the job on Wednesday and Friday I was paid. In the meantime, my friend was hired as a dishwasher on Twenty-Third Street for twenty-three dollars a week. On Sunday morning, I took a walk hoping to find a better job, which I did on Eighteenth and Third Avenue, for eighteen dollars a week, now with jobs we were real New Yorkers. By the way, the trip from Fall River to New York cost four dollars and fifty cents, a twelve-hour trip.

Now again I will back up a little, about the bed wetting, when we slept in the polish hall one night I was about to wet the bed and I woke up, that was the last time I ever had that problem. Now back to the jobs, I worked six days a week, Sunday was my day off, on those days, I bought a ten-cent loaf of bread and made myself a cup of cocoa and that was all I would eat on Sundays, I wanted to save all the money I could to bring home. Oh! The name of the place where I was working was The Coffee Pot, a Jewish couple owned it and when they found out how I was eating on my day off they had me come to the restaurant and eat there, that was nice of them. Well after two and half months we took a week off and went home, we bought ourselves everything new from the skin up. I gave my parents one hundred dollars and the same ten dollars she had sown in my vest pocket. After a week at home, we went back to New York and worked until Christmas. Coming home for the holidays my friend and I had seven suit cases between us full of gifts for our sisters and brothers and I had money for mom; I always sent them money until I started riding boxcars across the country at that time I was broke myself.

Now as I near the end of the story of my young years, I have to interject little stories I just remembered. When the First World War ended I was nine years old, and soon afterward the country was in a depression and many, many people were out of work, the city would give you only five dollars a week to live on, if you had a family that was not much. I remember there was no jelly, no butter so we would spread lard on our bread, sprinkle on a little salt to make it taste like butter. In our town, there was a dairy and each day they would give away the milk that had not sold that day, instead of running it down the sewer. Many of us would go to the dairy with a pail and they would fill it up, that was our milk for the day, and we were glad to receive it. Another time a candy distributor in town had burned down, the owner let the local people dig in the burned out building for candy, and dad went there and brought a lot home. He laid all the candy on paper layers and put it in the dining room chest drawer, then every so often we would get a piece or two. He had it under lock and key, if he didn't we would surely raid it and it would be all gone. Another thing I remember was this awful bread mom made. Every winter, mom and dad would bring home ten or fifteen bushels of potatoes for the entire winter. This particular winter it became so cold in the cellar that they all became frostbitten, so as not to throw them out mom would mix a little of them in the dough she was making for bread. It was awful and we kids would not eat it, so dad would lock up the good bread trying to make us eat the terrible potato bread and that didn't work, after a while he gave up and threw the potatoes out and we did without potatoes the rest of the winter, boy that was awful bread. That is about all I can recall of my childhood life so I will close part one here.

CIRCA 1925 - 1931
Age 16 to 22

I know it will not be easy to recollect everything about my life from the time I left home with my friends, at the age of sixteen up until I married your mother, but I will try very hard in this the second part of my life.

To begin with, I must go back to my hometown and tell a little about the first friend, the one I went to New York with, his name was Stanley Butko, his last name is pronounced like Butch—ko. He lived a few blocks away from my home and his family were in good shape as far as money goes. They had two houses with two families in each. In those days, anyone who owned any kind of property was considered well to do. His father and mother both worked in a nearby factory, which produced woven cloth. Stanley had a sister and a brother; the girl was very young at the time I knew him. I cannot remember her name, not sure, I ever knew it. His brother's name was Johnny, he sure was a fast talker, always had a lot to say. Friends would say Johnny, when you grow up, be sure to take up law, I often wonder if he ever did. His mother was a short woman and heavy. His father was a tall man about five foot nine or ten, one thing about that man was he could not walk at a normal pace, he would take four steps to your two and no one could keep up with him. As far back as I can remember I have never seen anyone walk beside him, he left everyone behind going or coming. Whenever my mom would see him coming she would always say, "There goes Butko "Butch—ko on the run."

Now on with my story, Stanley Butko was the first friend as I said that I went to New York with, he only was there for a few months, because when we went home for a visit, which was the fourth of July, I think the visit was a weeklong. Well, when I was ready to leave again Stanley decided not to return to New York so another friend came with me, Anthony Cyburt. I do not remember much about his family, I remember he had two sisters and two more babies in the home but whether they were boy or girl, I didn't know. Anthony was my age and his sisters were probably a year or two younger. The older sister was very pretty. From what I remember his father was the only one working, they never went to church and in a town like ours if you didn't attend church no one knew very much about you. Anyway, Anthony and I went to New York; I went back to the Coffee Pot because the owner held the job for me, as I wrote earlier. The Coffee Pot was on the corner of Eighteenth and Third Avenue; also, on that corner was what was called the elevator. Not as you know an elevator, it was what was called in short the EL. At the bottom of the stairs, leading to the El was a taxi stand

for two cabs, the drivers always dined at the Coffee Pot. The reason I am telling you about the taxi stand is because the taxi drivers were the cause of my losing the job at the Coffee Pot. I lost it trying to do a good deed; I will come to that later. In the meantime while working there the taxi drivers were always trying to fix me up with a call girl that lived up over the restaurant, but somehow it never came to be, you see I never had an affair with a woman, so maybe seeing that I was different the taxi driver didn't push it. I don't know, anyway, up to then everything was going fine, I really liked working there, the couple I worked for was good to me and I was looking out for their interest. One night as I was coming home from somewhere I saw both of the taxi drivers and this woman going down to the Coffee Pot's basement, they knew the owner kept the groceries there. So thinking there must be something wrong, or else why would they be going into the basement of the restaurant? The next day I told my boss what I saw, thinking I was doing him a favor, however I was wrong, for when the week was up he told me he would not need me anymore. I was surprised and walking home, I kept thinking what did I do wrong? After all, I gave him a good day's work, and I was looking out for his interest. After a while, it dawned on me, the favor I thought I was doing him was the reason I lost my job. Probably the taxi drivers told him to get rid of me or they would eat somewhere else, or who knows what else they may have told the owner. Well that taught me a lesson; I kept my mouth shut from then on. Well, I was now without a job, it really didn't worry me too much, there was plenty of work around especially washing dishes. However, as far as I can remember I always hated to start in a new place, I suppose everyone feels uncomfortable starting at a new job

Before I tell you about looking for another job, I am going to say a little about the surroundings where we lived. The house we lived in was red brick, in fact, almost all the houses along Third Avenue were brick and they all had stores on the first floor. We lived over the stores, we like that because when we arrived

home at night we didn't have to worry about making any noise, if we did there would be no complaints and sometimes we did make noise. At first, the elevator kept us awake at night because it was no more than twenty feet from the front room and the bedroom was just off the front room. After a month or so, we did not mind it at all. Fourteenth Street was half a block away and we enjoyed our walks there, it was always busy with people and many stores to look into. I remember Regal Shoes Store, those shoes sold for $6.60 and that was the best shoe you could buy at that time. I remember also a men's suit store that sold suits for twenty-two fifty, that was any suit in the store. The name of that store was Crawford Suits. We both bought our first suit there when we were going home for Christmas, after the purchase of our first suits we had our suits made to order at a little tailor shop on Fourteenth Street at the cost of thirty-five dollars and they were beautifully made. Also on that street were two theaters; the program consisted of ten vaudeville acts and a movie all for thirty-five cents. I often went there; in fact, that was where I saw Sammy Davis Jr. in his family's act. He was so tiny but what a showmen even at that very young age. As I sit here, a fur store comes to mind, because they had an odd way of selling their furs. The store was even with the sidewalk but it had two very large front windows up on the second floor and most of the time there were models walking in front of the windows wearing the fur coats. The crowd below was mostly men watching the models not the coats; I myself spent my share of time there. The models were pretty but not for sale. Oh! That street was lively with all sorts of things, always something to look at, and someone trying to sell you something along the sidewalk. They had what were called at that time Bushell men, they were selling things out of their suitcases, each had a little folding stand and set the suitcase on top and worked out of it. They sold neckties, can openers, knife sharpener, glasscutters, socks, all sorts of items. On a rainy day, they would come out with umbrellas attached to the stands. I used to buy socks, they were eight to ten pair for a dollar. I must say

these street corner salesmen were always on the run from the local cop, who walked the beat… yep, walked the beat, you don't see that now. Every time a policeman would be coming down the street the salesman would close his suitcase fold up the stand and nonchalantly walk away until the policemen was out of sight, then he would set up again. The reason they kept away from the local cop was they would never buy a license to sell on the street. Therefore, they stayed one-step ahead of the law. There was also a sporting goods shop near where we lived, in those days I went in for exercising and with my encouragement, Anthony joined me. We bought boxing gloves, the entire outfit; we boxed every evening, of course the punches were held back, then one evening, I don't know who threw a punch that was a little too hard and we were at it for a while, it happened that I threw a lucky punch which landed square on his chin. He was dazed and the boxing came to an end for that evening. We did continue to box each evening although being more careful of course. We both really enjoyed the workout.

Now again let me get back to the area, on that same street was a park, one block square with trees, grass and many benches where people sat and enjoyed the sunshine. At noon, all the workers from the nearby buildings would come to the park to eat their lunch. I remember many a day I would sit on a bench and watch the people. The younger crowd would always be laughing and they seemed so happy, talking and eating with their friends. I remember having fun like that in my hometown with my friends, here I knew no one so I enjoyed myself by doing things that I knew were doing me good like exercise and sitting in the park. Another of my enjoyments was to stand against a building or sit at the park and watch people by the hour as they walked by or as they were sitting. What a difference I saw between watching young people and the elderly, the young face was always happy, they always seemed to know where they was going and what they was going to do, but not the elderly, their faces were more or less sad. Even as young as I was at that time, I was always sensitive to what they might be thinking or feeling. I would say to myself, I wondered what they are thinking about as they sat there, were they thinking of what they did in the past that was wrong, or what they should have done and did not, did they make a mistake, do they have a family? I would wonder if they felt lonely, maybe I did these things because I was lonely. I remember also going to Times Square and standing next to the Capital Theater or the Roxy Theater for hours just to watch the people go by. I always enjoyed just watching, believe me, I never will forget that part of my young life. Many a day off, I spent doing just that, when my legs would get tired, then I would go to the movies and rest. Other times on my day off, I would just walk and walk for hours, sometimes fifty or sixty blocks; just walk and look, I got to know that area of New York very well. I loved walking because in those days I was able to see thing that could not be seen in the small town I came from. Yes, Fourteenth Street was full of life to me, it was Little Times Square, the stores were all lit-up in the evenings along with the theater marques, hundreds of light bulbs flickering, gosh it sure was something to see for a small town lad. As I said, I did these things on my own because Anthony's' and my days off did not coincide. Some days I would take a walk to the Bowery where the alcoholics were, that was also something to see; not from the point of glamour but from the point of why a human being would keep bringing harm and disgrace to himself. It was a sorry sight; there were not only old men but middle-aged men, lying on the sidewalk or in doorways. Some had no shoes; I guess they were stolen by another drunk who probably had his shoes stolen. It was the same winter or summer; they would sleep in the open, in cardboard boxes or other makeshift shelters. It was strange but in the midst of all that, there stood the largest diamond center. Most of the buildings in that area were old, shabby and un-kept. However, business went on as usual. It was a strange sight, between the two sides of the same street; one side represented the wealth in diamonds from all over the world, while the other side was human beings in such poor condition; the bottom of the rung on life's ladder, sad indeed; it left an impression in my mind that I will never forget.

Down in the Bowery you could get a haircut for ten cents at the barber schools. How it worked was this, there were about ten barber chairs, the five farthest from the window were the ten cent haircuts because that was where the new student worked, the first five chairs would cost you fifteen cents because they were more experienced students. I got many haircuts in the ten-cent chair and walked home in the dark because of it. No, I am kidding they were good haircuts. While down in that area I would stop in a small bar, get myself a glass of beer for a nickel and at the same time fix myself a couple sandwiches free of charge. That is a lot for a nickel, all the bread and meat was on the counter, if you wanted a piece of pie that too was only a nickel. Now, let's take a walk down further toward the point of Manhattan, the lower point. At that point there is a park called Battery Park, do you remember my telling you about a park on Fourteenth Street? Well it was not called a park actually it was just called Union Square, but this one is called Battery Park. This park was a place where anyone who wanted to get on a box and have his or her say was permitted to do just that, and many did. There was always an audience; however, I do not remember seeing any woman standing on a box. I didn't go there very often; I went to the Bowery much more often.

I have been going on so much with the neighborhood I have gotten away from my story. Do you remember I had lost my job at the Coffee Pot; well I hadn't remained idle, I continued to look for a place where I would like to work. Let me tell you about the procedure of getting a job in those days, along Sixth Ave, now known as the Ave of America, there were employment agencies and they posted job openings, all kinds of jobs, from professional positions to dishwashing. Therefore, you could pick the one or two; that interested you then go into the office and inquire about them. After you were told the particulars about the work and if you wanted the job you would have to pay anywhere from three to seven dollars, sometime more depending on the job and what it paid, although some jobs were free like the job I picked up after being let go from the Coffee Pot. I got a job bussing tables for thirty-five cents an hour including lunch, all though it was only temporary. You see I graduated from dishwashing to bussing but not for long. I soon found another job washing dishes at a high-class club, The Mohegan Club. What a place, they had more cooks than I ever saw in one place. The chief cook would walk from table to table talking to the customers asking how they liked their meal. From the beginning, I knew this job was not for me, the reason being, there just were too many dishes to wash. They had more dishes to a serving and a cover to every dish that was served, silver covers, so I said to myself this is not for me. Another reason was I had to work a split shift. I had three hours to kill every afternoon and since the club was on the west side, too far from home, I had to wonder around for those three hours. I would walk over to Madison Ave, sit on a park bench and look at the Metropolitan

Life Insurance building; that was not my idea of a fun-filled three hours. Once I took a walk to the Hudson River and looked out over the water, that area was the high-class area all right, but as I said, just too many dishes to wash. As for Anthony, he was working right along, I do not remember where though, most likely dish washing also. From here on, I will write about him as Tony because I always called him Tony, it was a shame that our days still did not coincide and we had to go it alone for a while. There was so much to see in the "Big Apple" I kept busy walking and looking.

After that job, I found another in a nice place, but it was only in the evenings from five to nine, bussing tables this time. I don't remember how long I was employed there but I needed to find a job with more hours, a regular job was twelve hours a day and six days a week. That was what I was looking for because I had to save money for my mom and buy clothing for myself if I wanted to go home for the Christmas Holidays and they were not too far away. Therefore, I kept looking and walking the streets, finding out more about the city I lived in. One day I decided to walk to Orchard Street where the push carts were, that street was really something to see, all the tenement houses were connected, there were all nationalities, living on Orchard Street; Polish, Italian, Irish, Jewish, many, others also. I remember walking slow and hearing two Polish women talking in Polish, I had to stop nearby and listen because I missed hearing it, it made me feel so good just to listen it made me feel so close to them. I guess I was a bit homesick because here I was alone in New York and trying to get used to being alone and living in the big city. I cannot say I missed Fall River I just missed my family.

Let me say a bit about the Push Carts, they were mostly Jewish folks attending them and they sold all kinds of items, wearing apparel, household utensils, many, many things, I very seldom bought anything except apples or St. John's Bread. I'm not sure, if you know what that is, so I will describe it to you, it is a long bean like fruit, which grows on a tree. It is brown in color, hard, very sweet and very good. I loved it and whenever they had it for sale I would buy some, as for apples, they were a sure thing for me I would eat a pound or two of apples a day, I'd walk along the street and eat my apples, or my St. Johns bread and look, watch and enjoy myself. Orchard Street was always as busy as Times Square and very crowded. Most of the people had just arrived from Europe, it was a poor people's neighborhood and they were all striving to make a living anyway possible. It must have been tough for all of them with so many different languages, but there was plenty of food for the brain, you saw how hard it was to make a living, which is where I learned not to spend my money foolishly. They had suits on their pushcarts selling for seven dollars or less. Other things for as low as five cents, for them every penny meant so much, they needed every cent to survive, it wasn't the land of milk and honey to them but it was America the land of promise if you worked hard and they did.

Well back to my part in this story, after I quit at The Mohegan Club I found a nice place to work, I was a busboy again the only busboy the rest were waitresses. I worked there until Christmas and really enjoyed it. The girls kind of liked me because I was a good worker, I always cleaned the tables as soon as the customer left and that way the waitresses would get more customers, more tips and I too would make more because the girls gave me ten percent of their tips, so beside my salary I was doing pretty good. Of course, I never knew how much they made in tips you just trusted that they were honest, anyway in some other places I worked the waitresses did not share. I was satisfied with the pay and I enjoyed working there. After a while I became friendly with one of the girls, she was a blond, she always had a pineapple bob haircut, that is what it was called, she was married and worked the counter all the time, she would let me kiss her but never would go out with me. I did not press the issue too much because I was still innocent as far as woman were concerned, but it was nice just to kiss her; she was cute and it made me feel good because I never kissed many girls in my home town. I guess back home I was considered an ugly duckling, so this experience was good for my ego I must admit.

While I was working there, Tony and I lived in the same place, Third Avenue; we still boxed in the evenings and walk along Fourteenth Street. I remember one evening I went to the bathroom, which was out in the hallway, as I was returning to our room I happened to look behind a folding bed that was in the hallway, there on the floor I spotted a bottle full of amber colored liquid. I picked it up and walked fast to our room, Tony was there, I opened the bottle and sure enough, it smelled like whiskey. You guessed it we ups and drank it. After a couple days, the landlord stops me and asks if I saw a bottle around the hall anywhere. I said to myself this man is nuts if he thinks I will say yes, naturally the answer I gave was no. Then he said, 'I just wanted to know because I left a bottle of furniture cleaner.'

"Sorry I didn't see it."
I went to my room and after closing the door, I told Tony what the owner said about the bottle, and we both laughed because we knew better, and besides we knew he was a drinker and his wife didn't like the idea so he hid his bottles. Well I just happen to find one, and Tony and I enjoyed it. It was prohibition in those days and you had to know where to buy alcohol of any kind, which we had no idea, especially since we had been in New York only a short while.

It was getting close to the holidays, time we started to prepare for our trip home for Christmas. Every night we would walk along Fourteenth Street and window shop and talk about the gifts, we would bring home to our families and discuss what we would get for ourselves. It was for that reason we stuck pretty close to our flat so as not to spend money and save for our trip home. We went nowhere that cost money, Oh, we would go down to Orchard Street, walk around the push cart section, buy some St. Johns Bread or maybe some apples, or just watch people striving to make a living. It soon was holiday vacation and children were everywhere and that always meant trouble because; most of them would steal anything that they could get their hands on.

I remember a Jewish bakery with its doors wide open, and as you approached, the smell was so appealing. I remember it well, it was painted green and there were two steps off the sidewalk to get in the door. I visited there many time and occasional bought something delicious to eat as I strolled down the street. I think I said this before but I must say it again, that area was the best part of New York as far as I was concerned and I always had an urge to go there and watch, listen and walk. I spent a lot of time on Times Square and seen a great deal of the city, but down town, Orchard Street, that section always will be with me. The packed humanity of different nations, how they communicated was a wonder but they did. One thing for sure the biggest gangsters came from that section. Another section of the city we went to and spent time was Fulton Street, where the Fulton Fish Market was, probably still is. The port was there and all kinds of fishing ships, boats, came in with their catch. It was another place with crowds of people and busy stalls along the street selling fish. I'd say ninety percent of the stalls were owned by Italians, they ruled the fish markets in New York in those days. Almost any kind of fish you wanted, you could get there, *fresh*. However, nothing came into or was sold out of that fish market without a payoff being made to someone.

Therefore, between just wandering around and window shopping Tony and I, little by little were buying our clothes and debating what to buy our sisters and brothers. I don't know about Tony but I was always thinking about the trip home. I guess I was like a child looking out the window and he sees his dad bringing him a gift and he just can't wait to get his hands on it, I felt that way about bringing them gifts. I had saved every cent I could for that occasion, so I could buy gifts for everyone and give my mom money because I knew they needed it badly. Every day this desire was on my mind to make their Christmas special. If you remember the last visit home was July 4th, and Christmas having six months in between, was a long time to be away from home, especially when one is young. I missed my sisters and brother and mom and dad, Christmas has always been my favorite holiday to this day it still is. As the time grew closer, we decided what we would buy for ourselves, as far as clothing was concerned. We decided that we would buy everything the same. We decided on, a blue pencil stripe suit, white shirt, patent leather shoes, spats, blue overcoat and a gray hat and gray gloves. I cannot remember the color of the tie. Oh! In addition, I must not forget we both bought ourselves a cane, that was a must for us... we were to play big city sports... add a little class.

As the time drew closer anxiety was taking over, the days seemed to get longer and so did the nights, it was difficult waiting for the day of our trip to come. We had already gone to the boat dock and made our reservation and picked up our tickets, the cost was $4.50 one-way and it would be a twelve-hour trip; we chose a stateroom facing the outside. I didn't tell anyone at home that I was coming; I wanted my return to be a surprise. Let me tell you what I bought, for my younger sisters, I got them a big doll each, and my older sisters a beaded bag, they were the style of the day; also I bought the older sisters a shawl each. Anyway, we had five suitcases full of items for all of them, mom and dad too. So at last the day came for us to go, we packed everything even our clothes. When we were on the boat we took all our clothes out of the suitcases and hung them up so they would look good when we put them on, we were still excited to get home so we just talked and waited to be on our way. After a while, we heard the porters saying, "All ashore that's going ashore!" Then, "All aboard that's coming aboard!" Now we knew before long the boat would be on its way. After a few more calls from the porters the ship gave a whistle and started to move, what a nice feeling it gave us inside to be going home and not going home empty handed, I had money for mom and dad and gifts for all, and to be all dressed up like a king. We had accomplished something we could never have in our small hometown of Fall River. I remember it was the greatest feeling in my heart, I guess because I knew I was getting older and soon I would be tied up doing other things and trips back home would get further and further apart.

As we looked out the porthole, it was dark, the sound of the water splashing against the ship was soothing and I liked that because I knew if the water gets rough, I may get sea sick, matter of fact on one of the trips I did get seasick. I will never forget that trip, I had nothing to throw up and still got sicker, so I kept eating saltine cracker just to have something to give up. It was awful; in fact, just thinking about it is not pleasant. Happily, I was not sick on the trip. After we arranged everything we tried to sleep but who could sleep, we were too excited. However, after a while, we did fall asleep and woke to the boat giving a whistle and pulling to the port in Newport

Rhode Island, they took off some cargo and took on some bales of cotton then we were again on our way. After stopping at Newport, we knew in a short time we would be pulling into the port in Fall River Mass., we would be home. We forgot about try to go back to sleep, instead we started dressing taking our time, because everything had to be just so. Finally, the boat docked and we got off with our bunch of luggage, grabbed a cab and headed for home, we went to my house first. I knew they would all be asleep because Christmas Eve is a big night, what with the seven-course dinner and then going to midnight Mass and it was about 2:30 am. I also knew that when I knocked on the door, whoever answered, when they saw me they would holler, "Stasiek Jes Tutay!" That means Stanley is here. That is just how it happened and it was wonderful to be home. I cannot tell you what went on with the gift giving because I really don't remember I just remember they were very glad to see me, as I was to see them. I can still remember that house, it was at 329 East Main Street, and it was the house we had to bathe in a wooden barrel, because the bathroom did not have a bathtub. I am going to tell you of an incident that happen, which I have never forgotten. Before I do, I should continue by saying that after seeing my family we went right to Tony's parents' home and spent time with them. Then from his home, we went to church, morning Mass. I think it was nine o'clock Mass, we went with our canes, in those days that was the big city style. When coming out of church a group of young fellows hung around the corner and as we passed this one fellow started passing some remarks about our clothes and our canes. I can't recall what he said but whatever it was it kind of bothered me, so I stopped kind of quick and just stared right into his eyes, do you know that fellow shut up all of a sudden and stood there meek like, then we went on our way and there was no more funny talk after that. Whenever I think of that situation I always wonder what went on in that fellows mind, it just seemed in that moment I had to do something, I just could not let him get away with it. I must

have put a scare into him and of course, it made me feel good.

The length of time we spent home was about two weeks, during which, we hired a car and drove around the city picking up girls who never gave us a second glance while we lived there. One evening we picked up a girl much older than either Tony or I, maybe five to seven years older, and as we were driving around we had a flat tire, luckily it happened close to a house, we asked the people living there if we could phone a garage. While waiting we were invited to wait in the house, I remember how very nice and kind the people were. When the tire was fixed, it was kind of late and the girl had to go to work early the next day so we took her home. The reason I brought this incident up is, we had stopped along the way and talked and every time I would put my hand on her knee she would start to laugh and she could hardly stop so I gave up and we took her home. After that, every time Tony and I would talk about that evening and that girl we had to laugh about it ourselves. I remember on Sunday instead of eating dinner at home we went to a Chinese restaurant in town; it was not far from the big hotel in town, the Mohegan, another Mohegan. We dressed to the hilt and carrying our canes, we really looked sharp. The dinner was very good and we gave a big tip to the girl who waited on us, we could see by the expression on her face she was happy with it and surprised. I will say we always tipped the waitresses very well, we were generous because after all being busboys and working in restaurants we knew what it was like; tips were the only way to make any kind of decent money for the day.

As the two weeks came to an end we headed back to the big city, we were happy because we had a wonderful time and had pleasant memories to take with us. After returning to New York, I found a new job it was somewhere around Thirtieth Street, the hours there were from eight to three. Working there, I gained fifteen pounds, I am sure the weight gain was due to the good breakfast I had every day. The cook who was the boss and owner, would make me three scrambled eggs, cooked prunes, and toast, he made me a good lunch too. He was a nice man not because he made sure I ate well, he was over all a very good man, small man about five feet six a little overweight for his height, he had a wife and I don't remember much about her but they both were middle aged. They had one child, a boy about four years of age; maybe it was a late marriage for them to have such a young child. They were both very nice people to work for and as I said, he was a good man. The restaurant itself was a little different than the other places I had worked. It was situated in the beginning of the garment district. Lunch was served twice with two different lunch periods. You might wonder why, so I will try to explain. In the garment district there were so many people working that no restaurant could handle them all in one setting, so there were two lunch hours, one at 11:30, one at 12:30, people who came in at 11:30 had to eat and be out by 12:30, no time to sit around and chat. My job was to have the tables set for the 11:30 group then cleaned and reset for the 12:30 group. Sometimes I could not get to all the tables before the second crowd hit, so I would have to work as the new people sat down. I remember one time I was bringing water glasses on a tray I had to reach over a customer and I leaned over too far and a glass on the tray tipped over and spilled over onto the customer's back, boy, did he jump up, the water was ice-cold. I was so embarrassed, I said I was sorry, and he was very nice about it. The boss did not say much to me about it, and he gave the customer his lunch free of charge. One thing I noticed was they never hired young girls as waitresses; all the girls were in their forties and married. I wondered about that but soon realized why, the older ones were always better workers and more dependable, but.... For me there was no little blond to kiss.

A few doors from the restaurant there was a food market, sometimes I was sent there to get something that was needed right away. Near the market was an upholstery shop and the owner would come in for breakfast at the restaurant now and then, even though we really didn't serve breakfast. I got to know this man pretty well, he would always have a few words to say to me, I guess because he knew I came from Massachusetts and so was he. Once in a while we would kid around with each other. This one day he came in and said he was not feeling well; he was going to go see a doctor. I cannot remember how many days went by without seeing him. I was sent again to the market to get something or other for the cook and as I went up to pay for my purchase at the market, there he was, he was in front of me and he was buying some yogurt. He turned to me and said,

"If you eat this every day you will live to be one hundred years old."
He said this with a smile on his face. I don't know the exact words I used but knowing that he had been sick a few days ago I said, well you don't look to good now, maybe you should go home and go to bed, maybe your time has come. Well to my surprise the very next day, I learned he did die, on the very afternoon I said what I said to him. I remembered what I had said to him at the time but

48

thought no more about it. After the funeral his close family came in the restaurant, I served them, and while I was serving them, I noticed they kept staring at me. At that moment, I did not know what to make of it, and then it dawned on me that he must have told them what I said to him. I tried not to look their way as I continued to work the tables, but every time I glanced their way I caught them starring. I was a little scared, I wondered what was going on in their minds, and if they would ask me why I said what I said. Thankfully, they never said anything to me, I was glad.

Now to tell you a little about the garment district, the buildings were anywhere from five to seven stories high, each floor was called a loft, and on each floor all sorts of clothing was manufactured. On the front of the building, there hung a large sign with the names of the manufactures and the number of the loft each occupied; there were hundreds of these manufactures throughout the garment district. You may not know this Jeannie but Rudolf

Valentino was discovered while working in a loft building, he was a clean-up man. I am sure you heard of Rudolf Valentino, right? With the restaurant in the Garment district, you can understand how busy we were every day. I worked there until Easter then I asked for two weeks off to go see my folks; however, I never returned to work there.

The trip home on the Fall River Line was nice; it was a newer boat all carpeted throughout, I call it a boat because it was not large enough to be a ship. I really enjoyed those trips, seeing my family every now and then made a nice vacation from the city. However, I always found two weeks was long enough and we were always happy to return to the BIG CITY, not because we didn't enjoy seeing our families, but the friends we knew when we lived there weren't around anymore, some were gone and the others had their own interests. After two weeks, we looked forward to getting back to work. On this visit, home two French fellows asked if they could go to the city with us, we knew them before but not as friends. The answer we gave was yes, if you wish, the city is big and we have plenty of room; they bunked with us until they found work. It turned out it was a short stay, about three or four weeks, one went home the other ... well there is a story to tell about him. On Third Ave, there were two small movie houses, which showed movies at the cost of a dime. The place, I found out had a reputation, it seemed when any young fellow stopped to see what was playing and looked at the bill board, chances were he would be approached by an old man who would offer to take the boy to the movies. This was the way they picked up young boys and do more than take them to the movie. Well this foolish kid let the old man take him. What happen there I don't know but the kid packed his suitcase and left our place. That was a big surprise to Tony and I, but the kid being French who knows and he was a good-looking boy. I have often wondered whatever happened to him, we never saw him again.

For the past two days, I have been trying to recollect where I went to work when we returned to New York. I know I didn't go back to where I had been working and the only place that comes to mind is Joe's Spaghetti House in Brooklyn on Flatbush Ave and Church St. I remember riding the subway to the station at Flatbush and Church, Tony and I found work at the same place this time. I was a busboy and he was hired as a counter man, giving out coffee and dessert. We continued to share the same place on Third Ave as it wasn't far to our new place of work and in those days it wasn't easy to find places to rent at what we could afford, beside we were happy with where we were.

I knew we wouldn't be going home again until Christmas so I started sending home thirty-dollars a week, that was the way my mom wanted it and I understood that a family needs money every week so each Friday I would send the money and a few words of how I was doing... I remember one Friday Tony and I had to go somewhere so we stopped at the post office and I wrote my note there, reached in my pocket for the thirty-dollars, put it in the envelope with the note and dropped it into the slot and we went on our way. The next week I received a letter from home asking if I forgot to send the money, I wrote back and told mom I did send it on the previous Friday, well that letter and money never arrived. For a long time I wondered what happened to it, then it hit me square between the eyes. I think the man at the post office took it; I remember I was careless when I put the money into the envelope and he was at the window watching me. At that time I thought nothing of it, because I believed the people working for the government were honest but I may have been wrong in that instance; anyway from then on I was more careful and there was no more lost letters or money.

Now back to where we were working so I can tell you a little about the place. I liked the owners very much and worked for them off and on for about three years. All together there were five restaurants we worked at between the trips home. We both were good workers and could hold just about any position and do a fine job.

The restaurant was located on a very busy street, with a good amount of foot traffic, so the owner situated the spaghetti cooking in the front window; it turned out to be a great idea, because as people stop to watch they would get hungry, great advertising. The restaurant was a large place, many tables and an annex upstairs, which served customers but only on the weekends when the place was really busy. On Mondays cleaning the annex was my job; I received an extra ten dollars a week for that job which I appreciated very much. I worked there for over a year and I had the run of the place, not bragging but I was a fast busboy, could carry many dishes in one hand and always worked close to the waiter, I cleaned the tables fast and set them up again so he could get more costumers; meaning more tips for him and sometime he passed me a couple dollars. At this place, the waiters did not have to give 10% to the busboy because we busboys were paid a flat salary. If I remember correctly I was paid thirty dollars plus the ten for cleaning the annex, that gave me forty dollars a week; that was pretty good money those days. We were still living on Third Avenue but soon started looking for a room closer to the job. The hours were 9:00 am to 9:00 pm; we had a break during the middle of the day not a very long break. Here is how it worked; we arrived at nine in the morning to set up for 11 am when the place opened for business, we would buss tables etc., then after the lunch crowed was gone we would set up for the dinner hours which were 5 pm to 9 pm. We had only one day off a week and it was on a weekday and boy it was appreciated. On that day I would go to Times Square and see a movie or stand in front of the Roxy Theater or maybe the Capital Theater just to watch the people as they walked by; doing that was always a great satisfaction to me, I don't know why but I did enjoy it very much. If there were good movies showing I would go to as many as three movies in one day; I would go to the first one at ten o'clock in the morning another around one in the afternoon and the last one at about four o'clock then head for home I did that so many times maybe that is why movies didn't interest me later in life. That is the way the weeks went by, working with a bunch of good men. I should tell you about the other workers, there was a young Greek fellow he was the spaghetti cook in the window, and Tony, my friend, worked next to him at the counter. Tony's job was to make coffee as needed, cut the pies and give them out to the waiters when ordered. As you know I was the busboy along with Carl, a German fellow, then there was Harry a Jewish waiter and Shultz a German waiter. In the kitchen were two cooks and a fellow washing dishes that was the lunch crew, in the evening we always had extra help. Eric a German fellow was an extra busboy, a clean cut young man always immaculate in everything yet there always seem to be something troubling him. He worked there about a year then left, after a year or so we heard he committed suicide, I remember feeling bad. Now Harry was a good looking guy and he had lots of girls, I remember one used to come in to eat almost every day, one day I guess he told her it was over and she started to cry right there, I felt sorry for her but what could I do, nothing. Then there was

Shultz he put himself in an embarrassing situation, he had a family of four as steady customers they were German like him, one day he was caught not charging them for all they ate, I guess they were his friends, he would order them high priced meals then put a small amount on the check. The boss did not fire him, which surprised all of us. They were good people to work for, kind and forgiving. The bosses' wife was a very small woman, I don't believe she was five feet tall, they had one son; I can't remember their names. The son was around eighteen or nineteen years old. They were a pleasure to work for. The owner of this and four other restaurants always came once a day he had a chauffeur to drive him around, his wife must have been my bosses wife's sister because she was also very short, and they always greeted one another in a very friendly way, he never stayed long maybe a half hour then he would be on his way, Oh! I must say something about the cook, he was a nice guy, one thing that stands out in my mind is that when he would ask me to get him a cup of coffee, no matter how hot the coffee was

he put sugar in and stir it with his finger, I would stand and watch him he would just keep on stirring. I would ask myself how the hell he could stand it.

Things were going pretty well, we were still living in the big city, and we were beginning to not mind the subway ride each morning, it didn't take too long and it gave me at least time to think and fully wake up. During the time we prepared the restaurant for the 5 o'clock rush we would always have time to spare, so I did a little wrestling with two colored porters who worked there part time, they were pretty husky yet I held my own with them. Sometimes they would get me in a position that I couldn't get out of and sometimes I did the same to them. I enjoyed the wrestling, matter of fact I looked forward to the days when they were working, we became friends and I would go to Harlem to a Speak Easy and even drank some white moonshine, got to feeling pretty good. I suppose it was bathtub gin or whisky because that was during prohibition, as you know. Harlem was an interesting place I enjoyed it. That was how the days and weeks went by with Christmas getting closer, I can't remember where or what I did that Christmas so I will have to go on to the following year.

I remember soon after that we made friends with a new fellow working with us and we all started talking about going to California. Before long we knew, we were serious about it and started to prepare for the trip. We started buying the outfit, high boots, Knap sack the whole works. In late spring we quit our jobs then took the subway out of the city, while in the subway people would wish us luck and some would say

"Gee wish I was going with you."
What encouraged people to say that, was we had these words printed on our knap sacks, "NEW YORK TO CALIFORNIA" After the subway we picked up a ride and we were on the road heading toward Philadelphia. I can't recall all the details of the trip but I will write what I remember which will be mainly the high points. After being dropped off in Philadelphia, it wasn't long before a young man in a Ford coupe heading toward Chambersburg picked us up. Let me tell you it was a tight fit, no back seat only a front seat so one of us had to sit on the lap of another; we took turns but it was really cramped. We rode that way for five hundred miles and believe me it was a long ride. As we were getting closer to the last town before reaching Chambersburg I happened to mention there was a girls college in Chambersburg, we hit the town about evening but not quite dark yet, we picked up three girls, and as you know there were four of us, you might have guessed what is coming I was the one without a girl, I had to keep the car company as the other three went into the woods with the girls. While sitting there I kept thinking of these young girls doing such things and so openly. They knew from the start what was on our minds; I guess they were thinking the same thing. So there I sat waiting probably saying to myself, why was I not born good looking? Later in my story, I will tell you that I was kind of glad and it all was for the best. Well finally, they came back, said their goodbyes and

we were on our way, I heard no comments from anyone about what went on.

Taking the Lincoln Highway also called Highway 2 at that time and running from New York to California, we drove through Pennsylvania and into Ohio. It was and still is flat country as far as you could see. It was my first time to see miles of wheat fields moving in the soft breezes, it was like ocean waves and I can still remember how beautiful it was. That was one of the big reasons I wanted to take the trip, to see those beautiful sights, to ride and absorb this beautiful country, even though it is said a young person doesn't appreciate nature; I think they are wrong I know we three appreciated what we saw. I think that now the young are even more inclined to be adventurous; some just never get the chance. As we were driving along we came to a pasture, in the middle of this great big field, we saw a cow and its calf, and also there was a horse two tone in color. This horse would pick up the young calf by the back of the neck with its teeth and shake it hard. The cow would keep trying to defend the calf and when she would the horse would turn and kick her then proceed in picking up the little calf; it was a sad site to watch. I can only think the horse had a killer instinct. We went to the nearest farm house to report it, but what if anything was done I don't know as I said it was sad to see a horse behave in such a manner I have never forgotten it.

Somewhere in Ohio the young man dropped us and drove off in another direction, now we were on the road thumbing our rides. As you can well imagine rides were hard to get with three guys together so we decided to split up and as we were picked up one by one we watched the road and if we saw each other hitching we would tell the person giving us a lift that the fellow standing on the side of the road was a friend and so the driver would pick him up also, that is how we got through Indiana and into Illinois and then into Chicago. We didn't spend much time in Chicago though I don't remember why; we didn't even go see the Loop. However we did walk along the busy Michigan Blvd and sure enough the wind was blowing across the lake, boy even then you knew why it's called the "windy city". We then moved on our way to Joliet, Illinois and there this trip ended. To this day, I cannot recall why, but we were on the way back to New York, maybe it was the hardship of the trip or perhaps it was a money situation. Going back to New York was not as pleasant as the trip leaving but all in all, I have pleasant memories of being on the road and I'm glad we went as far as we did.

When we arrived back in New York we applied back at the same restaurant for work, I was lucky I was re-hired but not Tony, I don't remember about the other fellow what he did but as it ended up Tony found work a half block away and we also were lucky and found a room in a building adjacent to Tony's place of employment. It was nice, one large room over-looking the back yard. The restaurant where Tony was hired was a better restaurant then the one I went back to but I was happy where I was because I had gotten a better position,

now I would be the counter man and in a short time I was the spaghetti cook right there in the window with my big white cook's hat. I guess I felt I was getting some place; I felt important and was receiving a little more money to boot. We had the same days off and that was what we had always wanted. Now we could see the sights together.

During the time we had been away on our trip my family moved from Massachusetts to New Jersey making it not as far to visit with them as it had been before; I'd say we went home about once or twice a month. We would go to Times Square, and catch the bus to Paterson. After a while they bought a home in East Paterson so then we had to also take a local bus to East Paterson, in fact that home was the home you kids visited often. After many months of visiting Paterson, we found a place where we could buy bootleg whiskey so the trip served two purposes. Yes, I did get drunk now and then but never so much that I didn't know what I was doing, and anyway Tony kind of looked after me when I did drink a bit too much. As the weeks passed and we saved money we decided instead of going home by bus we would hire a car from the Hertz people, they've been around for a long time, we did that for a while just how long I don't remember but soon we were saying, 'Why rent a car lets buy one so with a little more saving we did. We bought a used De Soto Sprite, a coupe. We kept it parked in front of our building. We rode around town for a few days feeling like big shots and one day the darn transmission was not working right, now the question was what we should do, we paid seventy-five dollars for the car and didn't want to spend a lot of money repairing it. I remember we talked about it and I came up with the idea to just give it away. Tony was alright with that so, on the sidewalk stood a young man, I walked up and asked him if he wanted a car, the answer was 'sure', so I took out the pink slip signed it and gave it to him, he thanked me and that was that. Oh, by the way the car was yellow with black trim, pretty good looking. Now we were back to riding the bus and buying our bootleg whiskey

that was the way the weeks and months went by. On our days off it was Patterson or Times Square, or we would go to the docks and watch the ships come and go. We would stand on the docks look over the ocean and dream of how nice it would be if we could get on one of those ships. It almost happened once but that little story will come later. It was just that standing there listening to the whistles of those large ships going and coming made one feel like saying please take me with you, but no such luck, so after we had our fill of ship watching we would turn and walk away with our hearts low. Believe me that was my true feelings. I always wanted to go to Europe but it never came to be. So yes, that is the way we spent our days off. We were pretty close friends and had some good time going around together, always dressed to kill, in the summer, nice suits, panama hats, in the winter spats, scarf under our top coats or overcoats, patent leather shoes and gloves. Quite a few times the police would stop us and frisk us for guns, but they always got fooled. Guess they thought we were part of the mafia. One other thing I remember about Tony that I never could put my finger on was, he always had a slight yellow color to his skin yet he was never sick outside a cold once in a while, but many times I would look at him and I would have the feeling that something was wrong with him.

Time did go by pretty fast those days and Christmas was again around the corner, I don't remember anything special about that Christmas, I do know I spent it with my folks. Now, New Year's Eve was spent like many other New Year's Eves that Tony and I spent together, we spent it on Times Square walking up and down waiting for the lights on the Capital Theater to light up, as I think back on it now it really was a waste of time, you walk up about four blocks then turn around and walk back, the sidewalk would be so crowded, like sardines in a can, you walk back and forth for about two hours then the lights would light up and everybody would go out in the street, stop traffic for maybe ten minutes then start back for home or go to a restaurant and get something to eat then go home.

We were two of the thousands to waste our time like that each New Year's Eve, but that was how New Yorker's celebrated the New Year, not the rich ones anyway. New Yorker's at that time liked to mingle together to celebrate occasions, it was sort of nice.

During the winter, we didn't do much of anything, just work and saved money because we were planning another trip to California, for sure this time. However this time we were not going to hitchhike, we would buy a car and go in style. Therefore, when spring came around we were looking for a car. In addition, there was to be three of us just like on our first trip. We had made friends with a Jewish fellow, his name was Nathaniel Levy, and we called him Nat for short. Your mother met him, he and Tony came to see us after we were married and gave us a mantle clock. I wish I could remember what became of the clock; it would be nice if I still had it. Well back to my story. Nat moved in as I mentioned earlier. Our room was big enough and less expensive for all of us with three paying. One thing I must tell you is what happened not long after we moved in. It happened on a nice spring evenings, we would have the windows opened all the way; trying to get as much breeze as we could. We pushed the curtains to the sides so the breeze would drift in fully, and with them opened like that, you could see the large apartment building across from us, and every window was open there too. As evening came and we were getting into bed I knelt down to say my prayers and while doing so I turned my head to look out window, which was next to my bed, and I spotted a couple making love right in front of the window... well I forgot my prayers and hollered to Tony and Net, "Hey look at that!" Our window all of a sudden became very small for the three heads trying to see out of it, and I have to admit we watched the whole thing. Afterward the couple got dressed and went out and left the window wide open. Then, I got this stupid idea and told Nat to go over and climb in the window and look around, which he did, he went right into the room. He spent some time there finally coming out with a suit case

in his hand, I didn't like that at all so when he came back I told him he better take the suitcase back, after a few moments of hesitation he did. Just in case you wonder, the woman was not married. Nat was very lucky that no one else was looking out of their window and saw him go into the flat either time; I guess we were the only ones looking out the window at that time. After the show was over and the suitcase incident was past I returned to saying my prayers, but that window was being watched very often after that, we never had a show of any kind again. We shouldn't have been looking in the first place. I will say a discussion followed about the free show, but soon we tired and went to bed. The next day would be a twelve-hour day and that was a long day. As the weeks passed and summer was getting close the urge to travel was becoming almost the only subject of conversation. Each evening the main question was, 'when do we go, when do we start?' We were all getting impatient to travel. We decided to start looking for a car on our days off, and it wasn't long before we found what we wanted. We found a Dodge Touring, black in color, if I remember correctly it was really nice. Now we had the car, next was to get some food together, that turned out easy, I'm ashamed to say, we took a little at a time, from the restaurant where we were working. We then had the car checked over real well, oil, tires, and greased everything that was needed to get us on our way. When all was set we gave our employers a week's notice that was about the last week in May, which was perfect, giving us the whole summer to travel and see the sights. The day to leave came at last; we were on our way!

Tony always sat in the back, he never asked to sit up front, I did all the driving, and Nat sat up front with me. Once again we headed for Philadelphia PA. The reason we chose Philadelphia was we would catch the Lincoln Highway, and head for Pittsburgh, five hundred miles away. I remember very little about the sights because I was the only one driving. I do remember the road from Philly to Pittsburgh was very rough, with a lot of very high mountains in between those two cities. I remember going through Ohio once again, the flat country, and then Indiana another flat state but oh, the beauty of the fields of wheat moving in the breeze, I really remember that. There was little else to see because the individual farms were hundreds of acres each, flat as far as the eye could see, of course you could see a farm house in the distance now and then or once in a while a man on a tractor cultivating a corn field, sometimes a bunch of cows eating in a pasture or maybe even a horse or two but outside of that not much activity, yet it didn't matter to us what mattered was we were free and on the road doing what we had been planning and dreaming about for over a year. We really wanted to see what the west was like and nothing was going to stop us this time. We were finally going to be able to remove our shoes and walk in the Pacific Ocean.

On the road we never slept in a motel, we slept always under the stars or in the car. As we were getting closer to Chicago, for some reason we decided to skip Chicago and go to Joliet instead, and in Joliet we met someone or something happen which made us sell the car and continue our travels on foot again. What or who it was I have tried very hard to remember but to no avail, so there we were on the highway with our thumbs sticking out but the progress was very slow, we figured out why, someone driving alone is not too keen on picking up three hitchers at once, so we split up. However, before we did, we first looked at our map and decided which town we would meet up in; we always choose the city hall or the main building in town as the place to wait for each other. It worked out well and we were making pretty good time, we then decided to try riding the freight trains, the highway was pretty good but we wanted to try the trains, we thought of ourselves as hobos so if one wants to be a hobo one has to ride the trains, therefore we headed for the train yard. In those days many old and young men alike were riding the rails so we asked a few question since we were new to that means of travel, and sure enough we were told that a train was being made up which would be heading west. Knowing this we

went away, but not far just out of sight, we were told not to be seen by the brakeman, because if your seen hanging around, it would be obvious you were just waiting to jump a train and if found you would be made to get off. So we waited, lying on the ground with our knapsacks for pillows and listening to the rumble of the boxcars as the train was being made up and watching the locomotive with its smoke stack expelling coal smoke and dust; we were close enough that the dust fell on us. I remember how nervous and excited I was lying there waiting to jump my first train, we all were nervous and excited. We waited and waited what seemed like a very long time then all of a sudden it became quiet and we knew the train was made up and waiting for orders to get going. We were told that when it was time the train would give a whistle, it was called the 'high ball', if I am remembering correctly, it was made up of a long whistle and two short whistles. Soon it was blowing loud and clear, the train started moving slowly and we knew it was time to get running to jump on or we would get left behind. As we started I saw twenty or thirty guys running for it too, I said to myself where in the hell did they come from, We didn't see anyone as we were hiding and waiting. Then it hit me that they were hiding just as we were. I was afraid I would not be able to make it, but it all turned out good, we got on and weren't separated. The first thing we had to do was get out of sight so we looked for a reefer, that is a small place at the end of each box car that ships fruit, meat or any perishables, they put ice in those ends. These cars were empty so the ends were empty also and that is where we hid. You have to keep awake otherwise you could be locked in by the trainmen, especially during the night. We didn't sleep when hiding in the reefer. One time we hid in a reefer that had oranges in the boxcar and someone before us made a small hole in the heavy wire between the ice and the oranges, so we were able to get some oranges out to eat. We really took a chance because at that time there was a heavy penalty if you were caught. I do hope I explained well what a reefer was, and probably still is. There were three things we had to learn mighty fast if

we wanted to continue jumping freight trains, the first being not to become locked in the reefer or a boxcar, second was being very careful when jumping the train in the first place because as you probably know if you try to catch the ladder on the back of the boxcar and by chance you miss you can fall between the two cars and land on the track and well, that would be goodbye Charlie, as the saying goes. The third one is, although we never tried it, but the hobos were doing it, which was riding the rails, actually laying down on the support rods under the car; you see when the train is loaded with merchandise and everything is locked up the only places left are underneath the boxcars, or on top, however on top it's very easy for the brakeman to see you and kick you off. You also could ride between the cars but that can be very cold and uncomfortable because the train may go two or three day without making any stops and you would have to stand the whole time. Many men lost their lives doing that I'm sure. We had talked to some men who liked riding underneath and they told us they would tie themselves to the rods to keep from falling off. I remember some of the men said they jumped trains just to be going somewhere, didn't matter to them whether the train was full or empty. They said that the biggest danger in riding under the car was falling asleep listening to the continuous rhythm of the train wheels on the track. Well, I bet this is interesting to you, I am glad I rode the trains in my life it was quite an experience which taught me a lot and I learned a lot about people too.

Now back again to my story, we were riding the freight train toward Nebraska, we liked it better than standing on the highway thumbing a ride and not being able to stay together, on the train we found an empty boxcar and we were together. Finally, we pulled into Nebraska, it may sound odd that I remember the town so well, I guess it is because that first day while standing on the main street alone, I don't remember where or what Nat and Tony were doing at the time, anyway while standing there this prostitute came over and propositioned me, she was a good looker and young, no I didn't take her up on it, I don't know why I had money but you see I had never been with a woman and I guess I was uncomfortable about it. Anyway, I said no thank you.

After walking around the town for a while we went back to the train yard to find out if any trains were leaving for the west, as I remember none were so we decided to take to the highway instead. We got a ride right away, and drove for quite a long time then the fellow dropped us off in some small town, he said it was as far as he was going, don't remember the name of the town or if we were still in Nebraska, but as we were coming into the town there was a small shed on the side of the road, I remember as we were coming closer we learned it was a candy stand. When the fellow dropped us off, we found there was no one at the stand, we looked around no one in sight, and well we decided to help ourselves to some candy bars. We were no more than two blocks away when the sheriff came upon us and arrested us. He brought us to the court house and told us to wait while he went to get the judge, so we sat and sat, it must have been three or four hours and no one came, I don't know what his game was, maybe he wanted us to try to make a run for it and then he could really put us in jail, anyway we just sat and waited. Finally he came back, he asked if we had any money, we said yes, because we did, so he made each of us buy a Greyhound bus ticket clean out of his state.

Right here I have to stop because I am getting ahead of myself in writing my story. I just remembered the name of the town all this had happen in. What kind of a writer would I be if I didn't stop here and correct this mistake? The town was Cheyenne, Wyoming so now you know When we bought the tickets, we didn't think that we only had to buy a ticket out of his state, and we bought tickets all the way to California, even now when I think of that I feel angry because that was not what we wanted to do. We wanted to see as many of the states as we could. However, we were off to California and the Pacific Ocean.

After a long bus ride, there we were in California, we got off the bus in the big state right on main street in Los Angeles. We found a room in a cheap hotel, with the windows facing the street. The street was crowded with people then, just as it is today yet at that time, it was mostly Mexicans and not a lot of cars. At night, the street was bright with lights and music from the shops, and there were many people milling around. We didn't go out the first night; not knowing our way around we thought it best to stay put for the night. We watched from the window, whatever else we did around there, I'm sorry to say I don't remember. After a few days, we gave up the room and headed for Hollywood. I remember coming upon the Charlie Chaplin studio, Nat and I jumped over the fence and walked around the prop warehouse. I spotted a pair of white gloves, and thinking they were Chaplin's I took them, how silly of me but at the time, that was what I thought and did. I wore those gloves for a long time.

Our money was beginning to get low so we headed for Long Beach, down by the docks hoping to get on an oil tanker and go out to sea. We came to a place where they were repairing two oil tankers so we decided to hang around until they finished. Then maybe we could get on that way. I guess we spent about two weeks going there every day, we would watch thru a chain link fence. We could see people working but they were too far away to talk with, yet finally one day a man came close enough and we asked him a few questions. We asked if there was a chance we could get a job on the tanker, his answer was he didn't know when this ship would be ready to leave the dock. The second question we asked was about hiring on. He told us they only hire through the hiring hall in San Pedro, so we asked for directions to San Pedro and the hiring hall and left, thumbing our way to San Pedro.

It didn't take long to get to San Pedro, we found the hall, went in and found a few men standing around, we went over to a desk in the corner of the room where a man was sitting leaning over some papers and asked, what the

procedure was to get employment on one of the tankers, his answer was a disappointment to us, he told us that only union men were hired and there were too many men out of work, in other words, small chance to get on. We left a bit sad. As we were walking and discussing the disappointment and talking about what we should do next in the way of trying to find work, I don't remember who said, "Hey how about joining the Navy?" Well off we went looking for the nearest recruiting station, we went in, talked with the fellow in charge and that turned out to be a no go also. Let me tell you why, first of all before we went in we had decided if one of us is turned down then none of us would join. I was turned down because of having some missing teeth and also some false teeth. It was the same at the Marines and the Army. In those days you had to be almost perfect, teeth, vision everything. Young men were eager to serve their country in those days, no more now; they didn't need college incentives etc. Well after spending most of the day in and out of armed forces offices we talked about what to do next and after our conversation we came to the conclusion it was no use hanging around in San Pedro so we headed back east but we would take a different route, we went the southern route down through Texas so we could go into Mexico, to see what Mexico was like. I will say though, that California at that time was more or less open country, lots of beautiful open spaces.

We were running short of money so we found an orange grove and stocked up on oranges and that's all we ate for a while, although a steady diet of oranges is hard on the system we survived. I will add that a diet of just oranges you become full of gas, so we demanded that if anyone had to pass gas he had to stay behind, do what he had to do then and only then could he catch up to the other two. I stayed behind many times. However, it was all fun for the front two as they looked back at the lone one walking behind.

We didn't stay very long in California that particular time. We headed for San Diego to see if we could catch a train going to Arizona in order to go the southern route. So off to the train yards we went and found one we thought was going to San Diego but after about ten miles the train stopped, we ask a yardman if the train was going further south and the answer was no, well that meant we had to find another train to take us back were we jumped this train and start over. We caught another one and we were wrong again and back we went, you may not believe this but the same thing happen three times; I think it took us three days to get to San Diego and by that time it was getting pretty tough not to be seen by a brakeman, who would kick you off or worse. We then decided to stick our thumbs out and hope for the best. It was hard but we did make it to the California Arizona border, there we were stuck, no one would pick us up. I'll tell you how bad it was, at one place a man with crutches told us he had been on that corner three days trying to catch a ride, after that story we decided to sleep somewhere under the trees during the day and set out at night and walk the forty miles through the desert to the city of Phoenix, we were in Yuma at the time. Let me tell you that is hot country, nothing but desert looking east, yes there are some Date Palms, I think they were Date Palms, I didn't know what a date tree looked like at the time. We would find a shaded spot during the day, lie down and try to sleep, but it was hard to sleep in such heat any length of time. I can remember how glad we were to see nightfall coming because things really cooled off and we would set off walking; we figured we should make the forty miles even if we only walked five miles an hour; It was so beautiful at night; the stars look close enough to grab if one had long arms. The air was so clean and clear it seemed a pleasure to walk all night and it was. After walking a long distance we came to a gasoline station, it was open. Seeing this we decided to stay there for a while and see if we could pick up a ride when someone stops for gas, it was a good idea but we wondered if it would pan out, not many people traveled all night through the desert, especially in those days. However, we figured what did we have to lose we were in no big rush,

plenty of open space to sleep, but no place to ask for food, that was troubling. I remember we were getting pretty darn hungry and there we were waiting in the gas station. Before long, a car came in to fill up with gas. While the attendant took care of the car I asked the fellow if he would give us a ride to Phoenix, he looked at the three of us, he hesitated for a minute then said all right. You can be sure we were happy with his decision and piled in. After riding along for a time we asked what he was doing out this way and he told us he was a scenery scout for a big movie company, I can tell you we were impressed.

It was dark when he picked us up and close to midnight when we arrived in Phoenix, we thanked the fellow for the ride and got out of the car, wish I remembered the make and year of the car; anyway we then had to think about where we were going to sleep the rest of the night. We walked around looking for a spot, we couldn't spend what cash we had left to rent some place, so we kept looking, finally we climbed into someone's backyard, squeezed under their back porch and slept there all night. It wasn't as good a place to sleep as we thought it would be because the night became very cool and boy were we uncomfortable, we did have some blankets with us but they didn't do much to ward off the cold. We were sure glad to see the light of day and we scrambled out from under the porch in a hurry for fear of anyone finding us and perhaps calling the police, being strangers in town who knows what would happen. I remember we cleaned ourselves as best we could and went to the nearest restaurant and we were sure hungry. With our money running low, we could only afford pancakes or chili and beans. We chose Chili and beans, thinking we would get our money's worth because they stayed with you longer.

After breakfast we set out on the road again, a road that would take us to New Mexico another state that was mostly open desert and hot dry days; however, I remember it was beautiful. While in New Mexico we visited a prison way out in the desert, no towns around, the prison was empty; it had been an active prison in the late eighteen hundreds and early nineteen hundreds, the days of the Posse. We walked through some of it, we found dungeons with door of iron, it wasn't a large place and it was falling apart. While I was there, I got the feeling of the days when the west was wild, boy I bet that place held many stories. It brought back to mind some of the moving pictures of Jesse James and the Dalton Brothers, the posse taking after them, yes I must admit it gave me a thrill and at the same time I felt sorry for the men that had to spend time in a prison that must have been hell in the summer heat. The thrill to me was that I was standing on the same ground that famous men stood, men on both sides of the law. One can only say to himself, 'If only these walls could talk.' We spent time there looking into every nook and cranny inside and outside and I had only one wish in mind, that maybe I would find something left from those days to take home with me, a memento of this old prison, what a thrill that would have been; but no it was not to be. I imagine hundreds of folks had been there before us and have had the same wish. Well with all our looking around we realized if we want to get to El Paso before nightfall we better get on our way so we did.

We arrived in El Paso in the early evening, not too late to walk around and see a bit of the town. It was a big town even then and it was too late to go across the border into Mexico. We had decided from the beginning that when we arrived at the border we would wait until morning to enter into Mexico, that way we would have all day to look around. We had heard so much about Mexico and we were curious and didn't want to miss a thing. I can still remember that enthusiasm of youth, we seemed to have had no fear. Those days were so different from today, today you couldn't do and see the things we did and seen. Since it was getting late, we decided to go to the police station and ask if they would put us up for the night. In those days the police would do that rather than have you walking around town all night or sleeping somewhere which might get you into trouble. We often slept in jails in our travels. What the heck it was just as good as any motel maybe not as neat and clean or as comfortable but it was free and that counts a great deal when you are nearly broke. They did let us stay the night, sometimes in the jails you met other hobos, you talk a little then hit the sack and before you know it seven o'clock rolls around, pretty quick especially when you were bone tired the night before. The police would wake you by hitting the bars or hollering, 'Time to get up and on your way.' You do what was ordered, especially there, you get up, wash, brush your clothes and get on your way. After leaving the police station, we went to a restaurant to have our pancakes and coffee. Pancakes were only ten cents then, in the better places fifteen cents and coffee was always a nickel. I found that when money was a problem, pancakes and coffee were the best buy because they filled you up. When Breakfast was over, we were ready to explore Mexico.

From El Paso it is just a short trip over a bridge by streetcar, it was early when we arrived in Mexico, the stores were still closed so we decided to take it slow and just wander around site-seeing. I remember we walked to the outskirts of the little town, hardly a town, and a girl gave us the eye and at the same time she would open her coat and motion us to follow her, which we did, every so often she would turn around and do the same thing with her coat, we figured she was a prostitute so on we followed. When we arrived where she was living and she invited us inside, she told her father to step outside which he did. She spread some blankets on the floor and she lay down and motioned us to have intercourse. This was a crazy episode, here we were all three of us and no one wanted to do anything, she took two dollars from each of us, we let her keep the money because we felt sorry for her, especially with her father sitting outside. I felt it must be very hard for a father to have his daughter sell her body to support the family. What did I know about such things at that time? The house was one room and nothing much in it. Another reason we did nothing was that we were afraid of getting some disease, plus we were all inexperienced. I still feel we did the right thing; we shouldn't have followed her in the first place. I was happy when we left. She kept the six dollars as I said, at that time six dollars was like seventy-five Paso's. As we were leaving, she came outside and a man in a uniform came by and started giving her heck, why, I don't know. Who ever he was, I wonder if he took the money from her. There were also two little children playing in front of the house in the sand. There wasn't a blade of grass or anything green, and the floor of the house was sand also. What a hard way to live. I am still glad we gave her the money; maybe it was providence that we followed her home.

It was getting close to noon and we headed back to the town, the shops were beginning to open up, they were small, I'd say eight by ten feet in size, the front sides were in two pieces the top half lifted up and served as an extended roof and also shade from the hot son. There were many such shops on the side streets; however, on the main street, there were shops that looked like shops in any little town. After they all opened up it looked like Orchard Street in New York because as you pass by the merchants would call out and try to sell you their wares especially if they thought you were from the states.

Before I go any further I must say that while we were in Mexico, the southern part of Mexico was having a revolution and they were hiring Americans to fly their private planes into the war zone with supplies, well with us dressed in khaki shirts and pants plus wearing high boots they thought we were Americans fighting in their revolution, so we were getting big smiles as we walked along, we didn't know about the revolution at the time and we wondered why all the smiles and kindness. Well, after walking around, seeing what sights there were to see, we headed for a bar we had passed earlier in the day for a drink and to set down for a while, I remember it was hot and we were tired. The bar was small and dark inside and we sat at the bar, I started drinking Peach brandy, even while I am typing the words 'peach brandy' I still remember the after effect. I don't recall what my two friends were drinking but me, I stuck with peach brandy and we drank for quite a while, becoming friendly with the bar tender, in fact, he was the one who told us why everyone was so friendly to us; they thought we were American fighters. We were getting pretty tipsy and the bar tender told us to stop drinking because we might get into trouble and find ourselves in jail and he didn't want to see that happen. You see he was a Mexican but he was born in the States he also served in the U.S. Army, and when he retired, he came to Mexico to open a bar. We took his advice, thanked him and left the bar. We started walking back to El Paso and as we were crossing the bridge between Mexico and El Paso about half way across we passed a group of Mexicans, some words were said. As I mentioned earlier the bridge was the dividing line between Mexico and El Paso, the Mexicans were on the Mexican side and we were on the U.S. side. There we were, saying 'you come here if you want to fight' and they were saying 'no you come here'. I don't remember how long that went on but after a while they went their way and we went ours. It was a good thing because we were in no condition to be having a fistfight, especially me. When we arrived in El Paso, we went to the movies of all things and sat in the balcony. With no fresh air and it was hot, boy did I get sick. No need to describe that to you, but let me say to this day I have never drank peach brandy nor will I ever again. I don't remember anything of where we slept that night but when morning came around, we headed on the road again for home. Instead of going the way we came, we started southeast going toward San Antonio and then on to Houston.

Before I leave writing about Texas I have to tell you a story we were told and what happened to us. The story was this; there were two brothers in this little town, one was the Sheriff and the other was a freight yard bull, in those days, a cop was called a bull too. Anyway this freight yard bull was a mean one, so we were told, he would never let a hobo ride out of town on a freight train and one day, I don't know how long before we got there the freight yard bull was murdered and they say he was killed by a hobo and his killer was never found. The story goes on to say his brother the Sheriff would take his revenge on any hobo that he would catch or any hobo that was brought to him from the railroad yard; he would put the hobo in his car drive about ten or fifteen miles out of town and tell him to get out and walk and not to return to his town again. The desert was a hundred miles, so there was the hobo at the mercy of the traffic, praying and hoping someone would pick him up because he would never make it on foot. The way I understood it he would rather put all the hobos in jail but the state didn't want to feed them so the next worst thing he could do was drive them out of town and tell them to walk in the desert. Any hobo who had to go through this town knew to go through as fast as he could and after hearing the story, that was just what we did. Another thing I always remember when thinking of Texas is, in our travels we carried two guns, one a 22 caliber rifle and a .22 caliber revolver. The revolver was always in our knap sack on the bottom I never liked the idea of having a gun but it was there so I had to live with it. I was always worried that we would get caught with it and be held in jail for carrying a canceled weapon. As far as the rifle was concerned, it was all right to have one as long as you carried it in plain view. Now, I must come back to what happen; one day very early in the morning as we were walking thru this little town, I will say it was somewhere between five and six in the morning, daylight just coming up. We hadn't seen a soul around for hours when all of a sudden we hear someone shouting for us to stop. We did and turned around and here come this heavy set man with his long johns on, a cowboy hat, boots and his holster and gun strapped to his side running toward us. He showed us his Sheriff badge and preceded to ask us a lot of questions, which we answered politely I remember and I remember we were plenty scared. After being satisfied with our answers, he let us go on our way. Boy that was the first time I ever saw a sheriff

in his long underwear running after anyone. There is another thing that reminds me of Texas that will come later in the story.

About this time, we were getting mighty hungry for some breakfast and we were just about out of money. We talked about what we should eat that would last the longest in our stomachs it turned out we only had enough for a cup of coffee and a bowl of chili beans which would be fifteen cents each. The chili came with cracker, all we could eat, and put in our pockets for later. With that breakfast all our money was gone so from then on it was knocking on back doors and asking if we could do some work to earn some food. At times, it was rather hard, people were suspicious and I couldn't blame them. When it became too hard to knock on doors we decided to hit the bakeries and ask them if they had anything day old that they might give away and I must say nine out of ten bakeries would give you something mostly bread. Sometimes we would be given French bread a loaf that was maybe two feet or more long so

73

we would roll it up like a doughnut and stuff it in our knap sack for future hunger pains. We ended up asking for day old cake because bread was really hard to eat on its own without some liquid to wash it down. Sometimes we would go to the back door of restaurants and sometime it paid off with a nice hot hamburger and coffee but not very often was we that lucky. I remember we knocked on the back door of a bakery and sure enough the owner said okay eat all you want but after you wash all the baking pans and there were a lot of them, there also were trays and trays of cakes and cookies, we sure filled our stomachs that night. Isn't it funny how little things like that a person remembers all their life? I learned that without money a person is lost, lost in a sense of security, lost in where their next meal would come from, lost in a sense that you are alone, all the people you see passing you; they mean nothing when you have no money, it's like they live in a different world then you. It is a very lonely place when you are without money. As I traveled and hard times came I thought about those things, many times as we traveled I would wonder, is it really worth it to go through these hardships, yet always when you arrived home not a month later you're ready to start out again, the hard times were always forgotten. I guess because life is like that, you fall, get hurt, get up and start again. You watch the sun set and you want to see it again tomorrow, because life is beautiful, you made it today and you will make it tomorrow, the next and so on. When it is all over you laugh at the hard times because you actually benefited from the experience, you've grown stronger and smarter.

We arrived in the next town late and decided to stay the night before moving on. We set off looking for a place to sleep and we came upon a railroad station house, it was dark and we saw no one was around so we picked up some cardboard laying on the side of the building and crawled under the platform, we spread the cardboard and used our knap sacks for the pillow and went to sleep, we did have blankets tied to our knap sacks to cover ourselves with.

During the night I remember it started to rain and the platform had spaces in the flooring so down came the drops on us, it was a light rain as I remember so we just pulled our blankets over our heads and went back to sleep. During the night, the trains went by but it didn't bother us; we were so tired we slept well, almost too well. I can't remember who woke up first but it was daylight and people were walking on the platform, they didn't spot us but we could see their legs thru the spaces and we were afraid to come out for fear of being accused of being peeping toms and maybe arrested, so we waited until the train came in and the people left. We then scrambled out fast, we were very uncomfortable because the rain had gotten us pretty wet while we slept, but at least we didn't get caught and we soon dried off. On that trip, we slept in some pretty strange places. I remember one night in another town we slept in the round house at the train station, we could have spent it at the police station, they would have obliged but having that handgun in the knap sack we were afraid of getting frisked and then we would have

had a lot of explaining to do, so we chose the round house. Maybe you don't know what a round house is, I'll try to explain, a round house is located in the railroad yard it is round in shape, because inside they repair locomotives, the center of the building is a large circle of track that the locomotive rolls on while it is being repaired, when the work is complete the circle of track which can be moved to match up with any outside track so the train can be put back in service again. The round house is really an interesting place plus it was nice and warm, kept warm by a coal stove. We slept on the largest coal pile and stayed warm. Now about the gun, we got rid of it a few days later, I don't remember where, probably in a pawnshop.

Back to my story, after we dried off we headed for the main part of town and our first thoughts were of food, but what or where with no money we didn't know. As luck would have it as we were walking through the busy part of town, we spotted a sign, looking for people to pass advertising pamphlets in the residential area. Well that was for us we needed the money to buy a decent meal, we went into the shop and the fellow in charge gave us a stack to pass around along with a sermon, no dumping them in the sewer, we will be watching and if caught no money. No doubt we were honest we delivered them one by one to each house for the specified hours that we had to put in. I am going to be honest with you, that was the longest day and I was so tired and hungry at the end of it, food was the last thing I wanted, I just wanted to lay down and sleep. I guess not eating the right food for so many days really puts a strain on the system, but we did go to a restaurant to have something, after all that was what we worked so hard for. You might ask how much did we make, well it was three dollars for eight hours work and it was a one day job so we still had to be very careful how we spent the money. We were still knocking on doors and hitting the bakeries, the money was put away until we really needed it because we were still in Texas and heading southeast where there was much open country and very large cattle ranches.

One day we came upon a little house, no other houses nearby for quite a distance, there were a few horses tied up to a rail in the front yard. We knocked on the door and to our surprise, there were four cow hands preparing their dinner, it was close to the end of the day. We asked if they could spare some food, we would be willing to do some chores for it. They invited us in and when dinner was ready, they invited us to eat with them. It was a fine dinner of meat, potatoes, and homemade bread. I remember thinking this must be a very large range because this little house was just a stopover for the night when they were working on this end of the range. After dinner, we washed the dishes and about that time a bounty hunter came by with his horse and dog, he had his rifle in a pouch near the saddle and wore a pistol on his side. The cowhands knew him so they greeted each other, oh, let me point out that he was an animal bounty hunter, wolfs, coyotes and mountain lion. He fixed himself something to eat, talked for a while; they asked if he wanted to stay the night,

"No", he said, "I have to be somewhere else early in the morning."

With that, into the night he rode. There were no chairs in this; I'm going to call it a bunkhouse, so we all sat on the floor, there was a little phonograph, I should say a record player but in those days, it was known as a phonograph. There wasn't any electricity in the bunkhouse so it had to be wound up by hand. We sat around and listened to the music, you guessed it, western music. I remember the room was lighted by a candle or a kerosene lamp because it was a glowing light, almost dark. As the conversation was progressing, they asked where we were from and after finding we were from New York, the questions really started coming. They wanted to know everything and absorbed every word; I guess we were the first New Yorkers, the first big city fellows they had ever met. After much conversation and the late hour we all turned in on the floor and went to sleep, it was a nice night for me because when I was small I always wanted to be a cowboy and there I was, I ate, talked and spent the evening telling them something that they wanted to hear, and at the time I felt eager to change places with them. I wonder why life is like that, a person always thinks the other person's life is more interesting, more exciting, their work is better than what you're doing. I think for me at that time it came from seeing cowboys in the movies, you admire them so you made them into heroes. But if you really understood what a real cowboy's life was truly like, how hard they work on the range most likely you would change your mind. However, the admiration is there, it still goes to them when you're young, impressionable and you're just finding your way in the world. Yes, it was an evening that many young boys would give a lot just to experience, Many times, I have thought of that dingy; poor lighted bunkhouse and how I felt at the time. Here I am talking too much about one subject I must go on.

As morning came we got up had breakfast, said our goodbyes, they to their work and us to the road. That experience has always been in my minds diary, because what you experience in your youth becomes memories in the latter years, seems old age you spend time in your memories. I think every person has three phases or three stages of dreams that he or she comes back to. The first being his very young childhood and then the teen age years, his wild oats days, then his married life, raising a family. The last stage becomes his most important. You see your joys and your sorrows. Now I must get back to my story.

We arrived in the next small town late; it was dark but somehow we found a railroad station, which was open all night. We decided we didn't want to go any further; we wanted to spend some time there. It wasn't long and a passenger train pulls in and all of a sudden, we decided to jump our first passenger train. We jumped on between the mail car and the coal tender. The coal tender being the little, I should say the large box just behind the engine where the coal was kept to burn in the engine for power. In those days, all trains were run on coal. So, here we were on a passenger train hoping it would start moving for fear

someone walking by would see us. It must have been our lucky day because we were moving and on our way. I must say that after riding on it for five or six hours we were sorry we got on in the first place, it was a local and stopped in every small town along the way, not only that but every time it stopped they would shovel coal in the engine and we would get all the soot. We would have to press ourselves as close as we could to the wall of the little hole we were in to avoid as much of the soot as possible. Soon we were sure that the engineer and the fireman knew we were on the train but they avoid looking at us directly. The reason they could see us was there were no places to sit or hide it was a standing trip all the way. We didn't mind that too much, what we did mind was the stopping in every little town. After riding all night, standing up, we arrived in a town by the name of Lafayette Louisiana and as we pulled into the station a yard detective came to where we were and said, "All right let's get off." which we promptly did and he took us directly to the police station and behind bars, so there we were. I must say they were good natured about it they even bought us Bull Durham tobacco, to roll our own. I better mention it was our own money we still had some left from the three dollars we earned passing those advertisement sheets around. After two days we went to court, the judge gave us five days but we were let go the next day midmorning. The idea was to give you more days and then let you out early and they collect extra money from the state and didn't feed or house you the full time. That was the way it was all over the south. It was all right with us to be let out early, although I will say we didn't mind being there too much the jail was clean, the people were nice... but when they say out, you go out and don't look back.

The next town, we were headed for was New Orleans, although we were quite a distance from there we head stories that hobos caught there whether on a train or on a city street were given thirty days in jail. The reason given was the city fathers were building a city jail so they would round up all the hobos and vagrants and use them as cheap labor. Being just let out of one jail we stayed away from the freight yard, we didn't want to arrive in New Orleans by train and possibly get picked up. We headed out of town on the highway instead. We also chose the road because we still had to knock on doors and hit the bakeries for food. Whatever we were given at the bakeries we shared but when it came to knocking on doors we each picked a house, whoever was lucky ate and who was not lucky kept knocking until he found a nice old lady with a kind heart. Because the food was always eaten in the house, you seldom received anything to take with you and share. When we filled our stomachs we decided to head for the trains anyway and the one we caught took us just across the bay from New Orleans. To get across the bay the train started to break up in sections and was put on a ferry, this was very early in the morning and as the ferry was beginning to move we jumped on and rode into New Orleans, it was about six a.m. as I remember. There were very few people on the streets and we didn't stop anywhere we walked as fast as we could through town, that thirty day scare really made us move. Yes, we made it without any problems but I was sorry because I wanted to see the town of New Orleans.

Next, we went through Mississippi and Alabama, two of the states that profess southern hospitality, I can't say that was true in our case, but I can say that in Mississippi it was the first time I saw peanuts in a shed that had just been harvested. I had gone to the back of a house to see if I could do something to earn a little food, I knocked on the door and a lady came to see what I wanted, after saying my piece she looked at me for a while, asked if I would take the ashes out of her stove. Yes, I said and without hesitation, she let me in and after cleaning out the stove, she told me where to dump the ashes, out behind a small shed. While passing the shed I noticed the peanuts, being it was the first time I seen harvested peanuts I stopped for a second to look at them, saying to myself, so this is where they grow. When I returned to the house she had a plate in her hand filled with food and gave it to me, she

didn't invite me back into the house so I ate on the back step while she stood behind the screen door talking to me. I am sure I asked some questions about the peanuts but I don't remember what. After I finished eating, I thanked her and left to rejoin my friends.

Mississippi is not a very wide state so before we knew it we were in Alabama, Crossing Alabama was quick too, and soon we were in Florida heading toward Jacksonville. I don't remember anything really about Florida except when we arrived in Jacksonville it was dark and we were at a passenger railroad station, and there in front of us was a flyer, by flyer I mean a train that goes very fast and makes very few stops. I remember we waited around a while and when we knew the train was about to leave the station we jumped on in the same place we jumped on in Louisiana, right behind the engine and there we stood waiting for the train to move thinking everything was okay and we would be heading closer to home any minute. Not so, the train pulled into the yard to fill up on something and while we stood there a yardman walked over and said,

"Get off and get moving."
We did as he said and kept walking right out of the train yard. What else could we do, but comply?

I cannot say how we traveled toward Philadelphia, but I do remember standing on a bridge somewhere close and looking at the Hershey Chocolate factory and I bet you can guess what drew my attentions to the factory; it was the aroma of the chocolate. I remember we stood wishing we were in the factory but knowing that was out of the question we just stood there and enjoyed the aroma. What I remember next is being in Philadelphia on Main Street looking at a movie house and wishing we had money to go in. The only way to get money at that moment was to ask people for it and that is what we did, asking men only but no luck so my friend Tony dared me to ask a lady saying, if you ask the first lady that comes along I bet you will get money. I took him up on it but he was wrong. We never did get any money and gave up. We spent the night there in town but I don't remember where. The next morning we went to the residential area and stole some milk from a stoop, we were given some day old cake from a bakery and that was our breakfast. We then, started for New Jersey where my folks were living; I may not have mentioned that while we were away my folks moved from Fall River to New Jersey, so from here on it was not far for us to go. There are two things I must add about Philadelphia, one: I never was in a city that the police wagon was on such a constant call. We could not help hearing it because the city hall was about two blocks from where we were begging for money. Two: There were certain streets where the homes were kept immaculate. The homes and front stoops were all painted white. We saw women with bucket and scrub brush washing the stoops on their hands and knees. Looking at the houses from one end of the street toward the other, it appeared like one house through a bunch of mirrors. They were attached to one another all the same height, all the same windows in all the same places. I remember I could not find anything different at all. The sidewalk and the street were as clean as can be. It sure was a sight and something you had to stop and admire, never had I seen anything to compare with that street in all my travels. That is where we took the milk, I think because everything was so clean we figured the milk would taste better, and it did, of course, being hungry made everything taste better.

Going from Philly to New Jersey didn't take long; my folks never knew when I would pop up so it was a surprise to them and yes, they were happy to see me and to know that I was well and home safe. I am afraid they never knew where or how I was because I never sent anything, not a card or any kind of communication. Sometimes I would be away for six months or more just bumming around. The last trip that I will be writing next I was away even longer and still I didn't write, I guess they were used to my not writing and didn't seem to worry. I suppose because they had both been on their own at a very young age. Mom came to America as a teen and stayed on her own and Dad was an orphan and spent time in the Polish army so they probably knew I could take care of myself.

I am sure we spent a week maybe two with them and then we headed for New York to look for a job. I went back to my previous employer to see if I could come back to work, Joe's Spaghetti Palace but he didn't have any opening at the time, all though he did tell me of another place at Thirty-third and Broadway where they did have an opening for a spaghetti cook. If I hadn't needed a job, so badly I would not have considered working there because I knew what the place would be like. The restaurant was surrounded by office buildings which meant every worker would be coming in at the same time, lunch time, so I knew it would be very hard to know just how much spaghetti to have ready. It turned out that sometimes you thought you made enough and everyone would want spaghetti and then other times it was the other way around. But the worst part was everyone was in a hurry because they only had an hour so they wanted it "NOW' or they would walk out, and the boss didn't like it when that happen. So you broke your, you know what to keep everyone happy, it wasn't easy I can tell you! However being just back from bumming around the country and being broke I took the job anyway, with the understanding that my old boss would call me as soon as there was an opening. With that in mind, I or rather we took a room in Brooklyn again, down by Flatbush and Church Streets. I don't remember how long I worked there, I know it wasn't long before I became used to the place, it was not as difficult as I had thought, I'm sure what made it easier to take was the fact that a lot of pretty office girls came in, of course that caused a different difficulty as it was hard to keep one eye on the girls and one on the boiling spaghetti. After a while I learned to only watch the pretty girls and made out fine with the spaghetti. Oh, I must mention that besides the spaghetti I had to make waffles, we had four gas burners for making waffles, and at first, many waffles got burned. I remember at that

time people were crazy about waffles. They were a 'new thing' back then.

On one of my days off I went to see my old boss, to see if he had the opening he had promised when I left on our trip, it must have been my lucky day because he did, although it wasn't the job I wanted, I had wanted the spaghetti cook position. He told me there would be an opening in the near future and asked me to take a busboy job until that time. So, being that I lived nearby and I liked working for him I said okay. I was a busboy again and I really didn't mind at all. Looking back I feel there must have been a reason I had to take the busboy position because one day as I was working a middle age couple were dinning and I started to notice the lady was always looking at me, after they finished the man called me over and gave me his card and said

'The first chance you have come over to this address.'

I took the card and said okay, and after they left, I took the card out of my pocket and read it. It was from a movie director or producer, which I don't remember but I do remember he was a movie director or producer from Paramount Pictures. At that time, they were making movies in Astoria. I carried that card for the longest time but never went to the address. Many a day I wonder to myself and ask myself why I didn't go. I know perhaps nothing would have come of it but the satisfaction of knowing now instead of wondering, what if? Maybe my life would have been completely different, maybe that was my chance and I missed it. There is only one answer I can give myself for not going and that is; we were brought up always being told look out for gypsies, they steal you and take you with them. Don't do this and don't do that, watch out for strangers. So I think that is why I didn't follow through. My parents were ill educated and had many superstitions some of which I had myself. I never saw that couple in the restaurant again, however I don't think I would have recognized them if they did come in. I can't blame it really on how I was brought up, after all I did have an adventurous side to myself after all I left home at sixteen and traveled across the country, I should have been able to follow through. I know one might say well what's past is past but curiosity is the thing that troubles me. Who knows the bright lights and stardom could have been the ruin of me. However, believe me I have thought of it quite often and felt sorry I didn't go and see what it was all about. Hey, who knows I could have been another Errol Flynn or Gary Cooper...

Now I must continue with my story. Everything was going nicely, I saw my folks about every two weeks and while we were back at home we would buy some bootleg whiskey and get a little high, well what else was there to do in a small town for fun. Once a week or every two weeks wasn't bad and we did have some good times. By now my boss was talking about opening his own restaurant, which would be four or five blocks from the one we all were working in, the one he managed. He asked everyone who was working under him if they would go with him when his place was ready and everyone said yes, from the cook down to the dishwasher. It took some time to get things ready, the building had to be altered and made suitable for a restaurant. The boss was very busy at that time running back and forth and getting things ready. Finally the day came for the opening, we could sense the bosses apprehension, the competition would be keen for the restaurant we were leaving was as I said only a short distance away, one would have to give something special to hold the customers and get new ones. Well the new place won out, we had very good crowds for both lunches and dinners. In the new place I became a spaghetti cook once more, however after several months, business became so good the boss decided he wanted to be like the fellow he had worked for in the restaurant we had left, he wanted to have his own chauffeur to drive him around. He approached me and asked if I would consider being a chauffeur for his family. I accepted the offer, I thought to myself it would be a nice change, no more cooking spaghetti, no more dishing out coffee and pies, no more burning up waffles, I'd be dressed in a nice uniform and drive them wherever they wanted to go. I was surely going to enjoy being a chauffeur. The sad

thing is it never materialized. I remember I was somewhat disappointed for a while but soon got over it and returned my efforts to the spaghetti pots and waffles.

Near this restaurant was a park, Prospect Park, Toni and I would get up early in the morning go there and do some running to keep up our physical condition and good health. We both enjoyed the run and it did keep us feeling good. While working at the new place Toni and I became friendly with a Jewish fellow, David was his name, and he worked part time in the evenings. After a while he moved in with us. We had moved into a new flat, it faced the street and was neat, clean and close to the new restaurant also walking distance to Prospect Park. The only thing that bothered me at the time was I didn't somehow like the people we rented from; to me they looked like they came from a tough neighborhood especially the man. However, being a nice room, everything clean I took to thinking I might be wrong. It turned out my first impression was right. In those days, we always had a vest that went with our suit and we always had a watch and chain to go with the vest. One day I put the watch in the dresser drawer with the chain, we never wore it to work, I always wore it on my days off or if we were going out in the evening, well on my next day off I went to get it from the draw and it was gone, I could have bet my life the landlord took it. He was the type of man that never looked you in the eye when you spoke to him. I missed that watch very much for a long time, it was an expensive watch and I never forgave that man in my mind for taking it. After that, I never left anything of value in the room when I left to go out. Now you might say maybe the Jewish fellow, David took it, no this happened before he came to live with us. Well to go on with my story, soon after the watch incident I became the cook's helper on the day when things really became busy. I had the job of cooking the steaks; I didn't do it very often only when the second cook did not show up for work. Tony wasn't working where I worked, I think I may have mentioned that earlier if not I mention it here, he was working in a

nearby place and David was working most of the time in Manhattan but every now and then when we were all off the same day we would get together and do the town as they say.

Spring was on the way again and we were getting ready for another trip to the west coast, it was in the talking stage and David became interested. We started looking for a car; I was hoping it would be a good car. Everything was going along until the week Tony and I went to visit my folk. When I walked in the family all looked at me with a soft smile on their faces. I looked from one to the other for someone to say something but no one did for a while, then I don't remember who told me, but I was told to go to the bedroom. When I did, I found Florence Lawzen, she was French, a very pretty girl which I had worked with when I worked in the local factory two years earlier, and her father was the foreman. I was only fifteen then and knew nothing about girls. Some mornings, she would come a little early and we would sit together and I remember kissing her on the face. I never asked her for a date though. Being only fifteen and stupid about girls, which I think she knew, anyway she was always looking for someone older, that was the feeling I had at the time. Well, two years later and there she was in my parent's home. What had happen, what little I was told or can remember was she had gone out and had sex and turned rather wild, she wouldn't listen to her parent so they threw her out. How she got our address I don't know and why my parents became involved I don't remember or ever understood but when it came time for Tony and me to go back to New York she went with us. We had to sneak her into our room. Being David was working part time I told him to go with her and show her the town. One day Tony took a day off and was with her that day. Every time David would take her out, he would complain to me saying that she was always flirting with anyone that looked her way. One day she met someone I don't remember who and she left. No, I didn't have sex with her, none of us did. She was a very pretty girl yet somehow it didn't bother me when she vanished, it was as if she wasn't even there when she was there, if you can understand what I am trying to say. It was a relief on my part because we always had to sneak her in and out of the room and be very careful when she was in the room, plus I didn't want to be responsible to feed and clothe her, so it was good that she left. In addition, we had another trip to the west coast on our minds and we started talking about it as soon as she left. We talked about it every evening and started planning the trip. David started getting interested as I mentioned earlier and wanted to go too, so we pooled our money to buy a Pearce Arrow. At that time, there was a saying when you saw a Pearce Arrow coming toward you at night. The saying was, 'Here comes two motor cycles, drive in between them.' the saying was because the lights were so far apart that it looked like a couple motorcycles. The model of the car was a touring and that was what we wanted, we knew it would become hot in the desert and we could put the top down and ride with the breeze in our faces. We worked at getting things together. The clothing we were not going to take along, we would leave with my folks, except David, he would leave his with his mother who lived close by. Little by little, we were getting our food collected, we took from the restaurants storage room, the boss didn't know. We took canned peaches, cheese, Salami, soap and whatever else that we might use. I know you would call that stealing, but at the time, I called it borrowing for the money that the boss might have under paid us, while working very hard for him for so many months. I am sure you see the falseness to my logic, my justification. Your right it was stealing, it was wrong.

We were about ready to tell the boss we were leaving again and I remember thinking he would be angry but at the time I also thought, the world would not fall apart he would survive with another spaghetti cook until I come back again. If I remember rightly, he wasn't really upset. So we were all ready to drive off in our Pearce Arrow, oh I forgot to tell you we did buy one, we each put up one hundred dollars. However, just when we were ready to go David decided he didn't want to go along, and he wanted his hundred dollars back. Now if you were I what would you have done? We had quit our jobs and were ready to leave. Well, what we did was we got everything ready and when David was at his mother's over his day off, we packed everything and went on our trip to the Golden West. David still had the room paid up for the month, and even though it was not right, we were angry that he said yes from the beginning. We didn't have too much money saved up as it was and to give him one hundred of it would put us cutting it very close. I knew he could well spare the money, he had plenty, to tell you a bit about him, he was I will say about thirty years old, always lived with his mother and never worked more than five hours a day. He moved in with us to be closer to his work and we only let him move in because he said he would go along to the west coast with us if we went. At the time we couldn't make the trip with just three of us, we needed four to save enough money.

Well I'll get back to our trip; we took the same road as before through Pennsylvania then we turned south heading for Texas. I can't say very much about the sights this trip because we were not out to see them we were hell bent for Texas, the wide-open state. The car rode nicely, Tony always sat in the back, Nat sat in front with me, and I drove. We had all the food in boxes in the back with Tony, I guess we had a lot to talk about, but what, God only knows, I can't remember any of our conversations, maybe because I did most of the driving. Once in a while we would stop and eat some of the salami and peaches but in the mornings we would have hotcakes in a restaurant, sometime our chili and beans, which we enjoyed so much, they were filling too. Somewhere along the way Tony picked up a little dog, he was black with a few white spots, Tony kept him in the back all the time because I personally did not approve of a dog on the trip, it was just another responsibility. Too bad I can't write something about the scenery along the way but the truth is I don't remember any of it. We never went off the main road into the backcountry to have a look see. If memory serves me we were always in a hurry to get somewhere and when we got there we were in a hurry to get to somewhere else. Our goal and destination was California and very little in between held our attention or interest. I do remember going through the northern part of Texas, through Houston and Dallas, they were the big cities of Texas then, although they were just hick towns compared to what they are now. We stopped in those towns and looked around, maybe stopped to eat. I do remember eating in a boarding house one evening; it had a restaurant in the back. The cost I don't remember but I am sure it was very inexpensive, we had a steak each that must have weighed one and half pounds, you were served at a large table with everyone else. The dinner included all the vegetables, bread, desert and coffer you wanted, fresh baked bread, farm fresh butter, I'll never forget that meal, it really was Texas style home cooking. We slept in the car or on the ground and looked at those beautiful stars, they seemed so near and millions of them. You didn't see any pollution in those days, I remember it as a very pretty sight one seldom sees these day, maybe in some places but fewer and fewer.

After those towns came nothing but desert, a very long stretch of desert, we did stop several times along that stretch to gaze at the vast emptiness, not many travelers in those days, at times we felt as if we were the only humans in the world, it gave me a lonely feeling, a feeling like you are a little pebble in the sand in comparison to the vast empty space. I remember one time we stopped the car and took a walk in the desert, we came to a halt when we saw a horse lying down in the distance, we approached very slowly not knowing what might happen if we came too close and frightened it. We found when we were close that it wasn't a horse but a mule and it was dead and swelled up from the heat of the sun all day. I took a stick and tried to put a hole in its side to relieve the animal of all the gas it had, the stick being blunt took a while to puncture the thick skin. My two buddies stood at a distance not knowing what might come out through the hole, I ran myself but nothing but air came out. I guess it was silly of me to put a hole in the carcass after all, it was already dead but boys sometimes do silly things. You having two boys you probable learned that for yourself. After that, we went back to the car and set out again on our way. Next I remember coming to the foot of the Rocky Mountains, there we stopped again. This is where the third thing that I remember about Texas happened. Do you recall back in the story I said there were three things I remember about Texas? Well as we got out of the car and looked up at the mountains I felt a wonderful feeling that ran through my whole body, a little of my past came to mind, my young school days and I recalled the sister (nun) in school pulling down the map of the United States and showing the class where the different mountain ranges were and the different places in the country and where they were located. I felt like I was in the classroom when she would bring the pointer to Texas and say here are the Rocky Mountains, and there I was, standing in front of them that was the nicest feeling that I experienced in all of the trips I took, I will always remember that feeling. Well, at the time I just had to walk on that mountain so we started for it and the further we walked the further the mountain seemed to get, the distance in the desert is mystifying to the eye, but we kept on walking until finally we came to the foot of it. We did walk a little distance up but soon we were too hot and tried to continue, we turned back and started for the car, while walking back I thought to myself, I wonder how many of my school mates would have loved to be here right now with me, walking in this desert and to this mountain range, thinking that just a few years back we were sitting at a desk and looking at these mountains on a wall map. To me it was a great achievement to stoop down and really pick up some dirt and sand from this mountain when only a little while ago I was sitting in class trying to cope with what she was teaching.

When we got back to the car we found that Tony's little dog was into our salami, that got me kind of angry and I gave the little dog a few slaps on his behind, well that upset Tony and we had a few words. I realize now, if I would have stopped and thought about it I would not have done what I did, but I was looking at the good salami all chewed up and I knew we would have to throw some of it away and that hurt. We all piled in, the mutt too and off we went towards New Mexico. Can't say much about that state it was more desolate then Texas, nothing but desert. In those days one had to be very careful riding through the desert, you had to keep an eye on the gas gauge and the water in the radiator because there were not many gas stations on the road, matter of fact there were no concrete highways just hard pressed dirt and it was always covered with sand blown by the wind. I will mention here that before we left Texas we ran into a flash flood, there were cars stuck everywhere the water was very high in the dips that were built for the rainwater to run through. We, like the others had to stop and wait until the water subsided a little. When it went down to about two, two-and-a-half feet in the dips we started to cross but at the same time a car coming from the other side started across too, I was busy watching the water and I drifted into his car coming toward me, and my front fender went under his rear fender and pulled it off, but in all the confusion we both kept going to get through the water and after getting across the other car didn't stop. I wonder what that fellow thought when he got out of his car and saw his rear fender was gone. As I drove, I would glance at the desert on both sides of the highway and I would start thinking of how vast this land was, how mean it looked and how man was afraid of it. Man knew he could not survive if he ventured to far into it. He knew this land controlled the men in it. The sun beating down was enough to scare anyone. Yet however, all those years man was wrong, that land was just saying give me a drink and I will give you what is in me. I will be your friend, I will let you not only survive but survive well. Then after many years man did give this parched land a drink and the land began to live, man began to plant and the desert lived up to its promise, green things grew. The land began to come alive with food for man and beast.

The last trip that mom and I took to California on the train I saw hundreds of those acres planted with food crops and alfalfa hay. In time, all that vast land will be in use because man lives longer and multiplies faster.

I see I have gotten off my story a little bit but I remembered that so well I wanted to share it with you. Now I better get on with what I have set out to do. By then, we knew we were faced with a problem that cannot be avoided. The money situation is getting low and as happened with the past trip it seems we never start with enough money to get us to our destination and back. I suppose that is the way young minds work, always in a hurry to do everything without proper planning. It was too late to worry about that, so on we went. We decided that Phoenix would be the point where we will have to decide what has to be done. With that in mind we decided to stop on the side of the road and for a little target practice with the .22 rifle we had with us, another example of youth's lack of forethought. We foolishly set up some of our empty soup cans on the ground and started shooting. Without thinking about what we were doing, we not only didn't pay attention to the fact that the spot where we chose to set the cans was on a little hill, which we didn't look over to see if it was safe. We found out very quickly as a man came over the hill and told us that his house was there, the shooting stopped very quickly along with a sincere apology to the man, we gathered our things and off we went feeling somewhat silly but also very relieved we didn't hit anyone.

I can't say much about New Mexico only that it was the same as Texas, more sand and very few towns, so we had no reason to stop anywhere along the way until we arrived in Arizona, there we came upon those tall cactus that grow as high as sixty feet, we did stop and walk up close to them, I guess mainly to touch them, after all we did come a long way so why not at least touch them. They were the cactus that can save you from dying of thirst if you are ever stranded there in the desert; all you have to do is cut a piece off and squeeze the water out to drink. I am sure we did just that but to tell you what it tastes like I cannot. I am also sure we spent quite some time out there, because it was really something to see and to touch.

We continued on to Phoenix Arizona where we must decide what to do about proceeding further to our destination, California. Arriving in Phoenix we walked around the town, we saw Indians selling their articles on the sidewalk in front of the city hall, women and men with their crafts spread out on blankets, really nice things, blankets, belts, jewelry, and other things. This was the first time I saw a true American Indian face to face; before that, I only saw Indians in the movies. I remember hearing them speak in their own language. At that time Phoenix was a small city, with quite a few black people too, and when you walked on the sidewalk with your friends, say three abreast the black man would get off the sidewalk to let you pass. I was not used to that in the east but that was the law there at that time.

It was now time to decide what we were going to do, we knew we couldn't take the car any further, the money was getting low; not enough for food and gas too. After talking it over for a while we came to a decision. We would go to a small town and park the car in a garage with our things in it until we return there from California. The town we decided on was Miami east of Phoenix, a nice small town. When we arrived, we found a garage and told the owner our intentions and he said he could find a place for our car. After the car was set, we took a room in a little hotel and to our surprise when the owner showed us the room; he asked if we wanted to see a girl. In about two minutes this redhead came in and stood right in front of me, very close, she had on a red satin dress nothing underneath, well what could I do? Naturally I ran my hand on her body. After a minute, she left and said if any of you want to see me, I am in this number room. I do not remember the room number; I asked if Nat or Tony wanted to go, both refused. Well I have to admit I was the one that went and knocked on the door, she let me

in. This is the funny part of the story; I asked how much, she said three dollars. Then to show you how little I knew I said,

"If you do not satisfy me would you give me the money back?"

Without hesitation she said yes, well she did not have to give the money back. She was the first woman I ever was intimate with and she was the only one, and only that one time, until I married your mother.

We spent a few days in that town on the two trips that we made there. I did see her many times sitting in the window of her room facing Main Street. She was a very nice young woman, I would say in her mid-twenties. Her hair was red in color with long curls. I mentioned that her dress was red, I was wrong it was maroon. Each time I would see her in her window it was not a happy face it seems that she saw no one, her mind was far away probably thinking of her folks back home, or her past life. In myself I gave her a name, 'the doll in the window'. This was early July and she always had her window open to enjoy what little breeze there was. Next day we got busy, we found a large wooden box, can't remember where but we packed everything we were going to leave until we returned and took it to the garage where we had made arrangement to leave the car. We kept our suits out to travel in; that was our last day there so we spent time walking around town. It was a nice town, not far was another town named Clove, in Clove there was a Copper mine, I think that is why 'the doll in the window' was in the first small town, because it wasn't a mining town like Clove, but had a lot of men too.

When the day came to a close we returned to our room, told the owner we would be leaving in the morning. Therefore, the next morning we got dressed in our suits took with us what had to be taken and got on a bus for California from Phoenix. I have no explanation why we decided to travel by bus instead of the car, maybe the car needed some tires and we could not afford it or maybe it was the buying of gas but there we were, traveling by bus. It was a

rest for me, as you know I was the only driver on all the trips that we took. I can remember a little about this bus trip, to start with it was a very small bus I guess not many people were traveling those days especially on these sand covered roads. The floor of the bus was in pieces all wood covered with linoleum. Why the pieces, I guess it was easy to get at the moving parts of the bus in case of a breakdown. However, with the floor being that way and traveling over these sandy roads all the dust came up through the cracks. I am sure you've watch movies where the people are traveling by stagecoach and when they got out the dust was all over their clothing? Well believe me and I am telling the truth our clothes were covered completely with dust. When we stopped at the rest stops, we had to brush one another off. It was terrible to breathe in all that dust, I tell you it was some trip, a trip you never forget that's for sure. Now-a-days we can travel in such comfort it's hard to believe people use to pay for such discomfort.

We landed in Los Angeles the same place as before down where the Mexicans lived, where at night, the bright lights were on and the music was loud. Where they only play music from down below the border and it didn't stop until ten or eleven o'clock every evening. Where you have to take part in the parade of folks walking along to see all the shops and hear the Mexican language all about you, it was fascinating. I always liked to listen to other languages, as I mentioned in the early part of my story I loved going down and listen in the Polish and Jewish sections of New York.

We had so much we wanted to do and see and not a great deal of time to do it all. The next day we took a streetcar to Beverly Hills. You see in my younger days I had a movie stars picture in my wallet and she was none other than Clara Bow. I am sure many young people in my time carried movie stars pictures; movies were a big thing then. So anyway, that is why we were in Beverly Hills to look up the house where she lived. After buying a map of all the stars homes and locating

where they were we proceeded to look for Miss Bow's home, it was not any trouble to find. The house was a Spanish style single family home, in a very nice part of Beverly Hills. I was tempted to knock on her door but I had cold feet so instead we walked around the block and in the alley, I looked in her trash bin and discovered she drinks good whiskey. There was no action around the house all the while we were there so we left. Sure, I was disappointed at the time after traveling three thousand miles and not fulfilling my young desire to see her. So, we went back to our hotel in downtown Los Angeles. We didn't stay long in California this time either we had to go back to settle with the car in Arizona. I can't remember how long we were in California; I would guess a week at the most. Back on the road again we headed toward Phoenix. When we arrived in the small town where we stored the car, we took that big wooden box out of the car and packed all the other things we would not need on the way home and sent the box on to my folks where we could pick it up later. Why? Because we decided to sell the car and since the

96

Jewish fellows name was on the owner's certificate with ours, we came to the conclusion that Nat would have to forge his name, otherwise we were in trouble because we needed the money.

After we took care of sending the box, via freight to my folks we were on our way to Phoenix feeling a little leery about the signature deal. When we arrived in Phoenix and located a dealer who was willing to give us three hundred and thirty dollars for the car, we accepted, then came the signing, he looked at it and said nothing and gave us the money in cash so off we went. Now we felt really stranded but had no choice, back to Miami Arizona we had to get. Going back we went through the Apache Trail that was the name at that time, I see on the map now it is called Apache Junction. Traveling along that road was the most beautiful picture a person could have taken with a camera. As I think of it now I will try to let you see through my eyes the things I saw. This trail, a dirt road; was cut from a mountainside. Most of it was a one-car lane. As you traveled from Phoenix to Miami, it was all an uphill climb. Coming around a bend you came to a beautiful view of the valley below, let's say five hundred feet below. There in this valley was an Indian settlement, all wigwams, fires outside, children riding horses, scenes you only see in the movies. We had to stop and look upon this once in a lifetime scene, I'll never forget how beautiful it was. Never having seen the true Indian and how they lived, only seeing movies where the Indian was always portrayed as the bad guy it made me a little uneasy and sad. Looking down on them on this lonely road, thinking would they come up and try to scalp us? I know that kind of thinking was farfetched but being a kid from a small town a thought like that is not peculiar. I wish I had taken a picture of the valley. I guess the eye sees it but the young mind does not appreciate what it is seeing. As I think back now and count the years, it's been sixty two years since I saw the Indian with their primitive way of riding horse bareback, walking to the stream that ran near their camp for water, Indians walking from wigwam to wigwam visiting.

We stood there and took all this in with surprise. This beautiful picture died with time never to reappear except in old movies and museums. As we walked along the road toward our destination, every few steps we would look back to be sure we didn't miss anything until it was out of sight.

Along this same road, we were given a ride to our destination. Miami was the first town you came to and it was not long and we were there, we thanked the driver and got out. Now that we had three hundred dollars we were in good shape for a while, what we did was we split the money; each of us had one hundred and ten dollars. After getting a hotel room we decided to try to get a job on a ranch where they might need hired hands and we could learn to be cowpunchers. Every kid wants to be a cowboy and we were in a good position to try. Not in a hurry, though we wanted to spend a few days around town. We found out there was to be a dance on that Saturday night in the town hall. So, we decided to attend. It turned out it was where folks from all around gathered and raised heck. So come Saturday night we got dressed and went. I know I felt a little out of place because the locals could spot a new comer right away and we were three new comers, so we kept to ourselves. We had never danced with a girl anyway and I was not about to try. The girls were looking our way a lot but I think it was curiosity that had them looking. After a while the hall became pretty crowded and the western music started and the dance began. All the cowboys were dressed in their western suits and new hats and new boots, I guess that is the only time they get a chance to show off their suits is at a town dance, or maybe church. The girls were in their summer dresses, nothing fancy, none wore long western dresses like you see in the movies, well I'll get back to the dance, it was pretty lively all evening and as the dance was getting near its end someone would sneak and pull the main switch and the place would be dark, then you would hear a few yahoos. I guess they would do their kissing then, this would go on a few times and then the dance would come to an end. Some guys would leave with the girls they met and some like us would leave empty handed. Nat had one dance with a girl but that was all. Back to the hotel, we went wishing we had danced.

The next day we decided to look for a job on a ranch but to do that we had to do it the right way; we went to a western store and bought everything that would make us look like cowboys. We bought boots, Levis, a hat, spurs and shirts. The ranch that we were to contact was fifteen miles from town so the following day we got dressed and started to walk. It was a pretty warm day, we got a little ways out of town on a dirt road, well not being used to walking in high heel boots and their being brand new, it wasn't long and our feet were hurting, but no turning back. After a time I had to take my boots off and try to walk without them, I'm telling you it was torture. There was not a chance of getting a ride because it was a back county road and not many cars go by. After walking about seven or eight miles we came to a creek, man was that a sight for sore feet! I could not get there fast

enough, off came the socks and into the water, my feet went. There we sat for a good while and I noticed my heels were red and the toes also, but like I wrote before, there was no turning back I wanted to be a cowboy, every kids dream and I was no different. At the creek was a nice spot to stay especially for our feet, but we had to move on if we wanted to reach the ranch before dark. Our feet became so bad we even tried carrying each other piggyback for a stretch, anything to help our feet. Well we did make it to the ranch and talked with the owner but he couldn't use us, we even offered to work for free but the answer was still no, I suppose he knew we would be more trouble than help. He did tell us to stay for dinner and spend the night in the bunkhouse. While there we met his son and the son fell in love with my spurs, they were solid silver; he wanted to give me his horse in trade. What the hell could I do with a horse so I declined his offer. I did ask if I could ride his horse and he said I could. Now, clearly this was the first time I was going to sit on a horse in my life, never mind try to ride it.

However, I got on and I directed the horse towards the house and this damn house took off for the barn. I'm hollering ho! And he's not listening to me he keeps on going, I can see the barn getting closer and if I don't stop him he will go through that door and I will be on my fanny and possibly get hurt. I was saying to myself, 'you got to stop this darn horse!' or your face is going to hit the side of the barn. Then I dug my feet in the stirrups and pulled as hard as I could on his reigns, he came to a stop about six feet from the barn. I got off the son-of-a-gun and walked him back to his owner. I think the boy knew what the horse would do and wanted to see what I would do. We all had a good laugh anyway, well not me so much. When it came time for dinner we ate in the main house and slept with the rest of the ranch hands in the bunkhouse. In the morning back to town sore feet or no and back to the store to sell what we bought for less money than we paid, as for me that was the end of the cowboy dream. While returning to the hotel Tony and I had some words, I don't remember about what but I do remember it became very heated, and as we entered the hotel fists started flying, with the commotion we had made the owner came over but by then it was all over and we told him it was nothing and he left. In our room the three of us talked about what we were going to do next, Nat and I decided to go back to California and Tony decided he was going back east, so here we parted ways. I really can't remember if the fight was the reason Tony decided to return east, but I feel it was. Nat and I set off the following morning and after traveling through Arizona and into the desert of California we became acquainted with a young fellow, he was about seventeen, he told us he was an orphan and that he left the home because he wanted to see the country. He stayed with us; I guess he kind of adopted us and we did him. I don't remember his name but William seems to fit the memory I have of him, so that will be his name in the story. I will call him Willy for short.

We traveled by train this time and landed in Long Beach, and that is where we made our home for a pretty long time.

The city was only seven blocks of businesses and they were located on American Ave, the main street at that time. There was nothing at all on the oceanfront except one theater. We made our home on Seventh Street next to the water front, and built ourselves a place to sleep on the beach out of old railroad ties, there we ate, slept and watched the ocean, also there, is where we tried to figure out what to do to earn some money, because we had so little left. As you can imagine the weather was always nice and every morning we would go to the foot of American Ave and get wet, I didn't know how to swim so I wouldn't go into the ocean, but there was a large hole on the beach and when the tide was high it would fill up and that is where I would be, I wasn't afraid to walk in there and after a while I found I was able to float, as I said we would do that every day. The distance from our make-shift sleeping area to the watering hole was about half-a-block and very near the water hole was a large sailing ship that the movie industry used to make movies, it was really quite large as I said, one of the pictures made on it was Moby Dick, not the one with Gregory Peck, a much earlier version. Also made on that ship were The Three Musketeers, pictures with Errol Flynn, Douglas Fairbanks and maybe even Gregory Peck in the 50's. We sneaked upon it often and walked all over looking at everything. It was an actual old ship and being in the water it creaked and I remember it giving me an eerie feeling, it brought to mind pirates in action, and at the same time a good feeling that I was standing on a real ship that was also used in making movies. Living so near, it was always something to look at and think about, your eyes always seem to wonder over to it and your imagination would come up with all sort of dreams. Another thing that was near was the taxi boat that took folks to the gambling boat, which was three miles off shore, beyond the government jurisdiction. We went out to it several times but never won any money, we always lost so we soon tired of that. Between the swimming hole and our visits to the gambling boat, life wasn't bad at that point. The weather was beautiful so what more could a person ask, although it wasn't long and the money ran out, however before it ran out completely we bought a ten quart pail which we took to the market, we went to different stalls and asked for whatever they were selling, for instance, vegetables, meat, things we could put in our pail with water and over a fire make ourselves Mulligan stew. If I remember correctly, it was really tasty and nourishing. We ate a lot of Mulligan stew, which is how we survived for many days. That was all we could do because there wasn't any use looking for work, there wasn't any to be found. Plus at that time, things were very hard in California, and to be able to get work you had to be born in the state and you had to carry your birth certificate with you and show it. Things were so bad that the state would give anyone that would leave ten dollars and a tank full of gas. We could not leave, we didn't have a car and they would not give us the ten dollars, but one-day lady luck did shine on us, I should say me. We went to market and I approached someone at the fruit stand, it happened he was not the boss but he pointed out the boss of the market to me. I went and asked for some things to make our Mulligan stew and he asked if we would be willing to help load a truck with fruit that was to go into cold storage, if so he would give us enough money to go to a restaurant for a meal. We jumped at the chance.

The lugs we were to load on the truck were wooden boxes filled with fruit, grapes, apricots, peaches, pears, apples and oranges. Each lug weighed about twenty to thirty pounds if I remember correctly. I remember the boss was sitting in one of the stalls watching us, and of course being young I was pretty strong; I would pick up two to three boxes at a time and carry them to the truck at the curb. We all worked fast and hard anticipating the restaurant meal we were going to have. When we finished, he was true to his word and gave us a few dollars, enough to get three good meals and have change left. When he paid us, he asked if I would be willing to drive the truck and he would hire Nat and Willy to help unload the fruit. I told him I didn't have a California driver's license. He said, "Don't worry about that." This all happened on a Saturday evening which meant Monday we had jobs, and we would be staying in California for a while, which is what we wanted to do all along. We also knew it would be the last two nights we would be sleeping on the beach among railroad ties. We all slept well that night. The next day, Sunday, we spent on the beach. Nat spent a lot of time swimming while we were in Long Beach, I don't remember if Willy swam, in fact I don't remember if he knew how to swim, and of course as I said I didn't, so I either floated in the swimming hole or roamed around the beach and the pirate ship.

Come Monday morning we reported to work at the bosses house, I would say it was about five miles from town, don't ask me how we got there, it could have been that the boss sent someone to pick us up, I don't remember. Anyway we got there and before I jumped into the truck the boss gave me a badge to pin on the cap I was to wear, the badge represented a California driver's license, he also told

me the first chance I had I was to go get a license, which I did. So now we were working, the boss sent one of his men along with me on the first day to show me where the cold storage house was, I remember it was a good size building. I should tell you a bit about the storage building. It was large as I said, inside it was made up of little rooms, divided by chicken wire, that way the whole area could be kept cool by one cooling unit. All the fruit and vegetable keepers rented one or two of the little rooms where they stored their perishables. My job was to bring what was needed from storage in the early morning to market then return what wasn't needed or sold at the end of the day. Many times my boss would go to the grape growers and buy a hundred or two lugs of grapes or other fruit and I would load them and take them to storage. It wasn't a bad job, the trucking back and forth was my only job while Nat and Willy worked in the stalls unless I needed help then I would take one of them with me. We rented a room close by, maybe a block away.

There is so much to write about of that time I hope I do a good job. First, I will tell you about the people we were working with. Besides Nat, Willy and I, there were three other workers, two brothers and the driver of the truck, by the way he was not fired when I took over his job, he was an older man so I suppose that is the reason I was given his job. The two brothers were younger, all though not as young as us, so all together there were six of us. The market area was quite large; also in the area was a meat market, a large grocery department, a delicatessen and an ice cream counter that served light meals. Now to tell you a little about the boss, he was a big man maybe weighed about two hundred and forty/fifty pounds, I'm not a good judge of weight so give or take ten to twenty pounds. He was well dressed and never did any work; he sat at the market counter all day unless he had somewhere to go. He knew everybody in town, and very into political matters, there was always someone stopping by to sit and talk with him. He also always had silver dollars in his hand and he would play with them whether talking with someone of just sitting alone. I remember him as a good and just man; I really liked him. Mr. A. H. Anderson was his name and his family consisted of three daughters, two of them were still in school, the eldest was, I would say about twenty-five, the next was seventeen/eighteen and the youngest about fifteen. The only name I remember of the three was the middle one her name was Mary. She kind of liked me and for my birthday, she bought me a silk T-shirt blue in color. I really didn't care for any of the girls they were all too over-weight. However, we were told in so many words hands off the girls. We worked for him for quite a while and only once did we get the okay to take the girls to a movie with the older girl going too. The younger girls set that up we didn't. The older girl seldom talked to the father or the mother, the reason I could never figure out, I think she was a step-mother so perhaps that was the reason the girl didn't talk much, all though the mother seemed nice enough to me but who knows what goes on at home.

As I said before, we had taken a room nearby, but Willy who didn't have any money, the boss let him sleep in the garage until he received his first pay check then he was to get a room too. Every week on Tuesday and Thursday the city would let all who wanted, to set up their stalls around the city park and sell their wares. Oh, sure they had to pay for the privilege of course. On those days, we had to get up about five am and with orders from the day before as to just what fruit to bring from the store and storage unit. We would load them in the stall and sit under the canvas roof to keep the sun from our heads and the fruit. We would get there as early as we could to have everything ready by eight a.m.. Our boss had two stalls to set up and the selling time was about four hours in all, then we had to take everything down and back to the store and storage unit. One thing I remember noticing while I was there was, that the people selling flowers always were sold out before the food stalls, even though the times were pretty lean, people had to have flowers I guess but at the time it always amazed me; why would a person buy flowers and not food? However, on the other hand maybe the folks that bought flowers were well to do, or they wanted to starve to death smelling flowers.

Everything went well for several weeks and then one day we asked the boss if we could have the truck and stay in town until it was time to go home, he said okay. We did not use the truck to go anywhere it was only to get home at night. After all the gas those days was ten cents a gallon, Willy hadn't gotten a room as yet and the boss didn't mind his sleeping in the garage and Willy wanted to save money so after work he would go with us down to the beach or to the movie and after that we would go to a restaurant for a little something to eat then home. On weekends, though the big thing was dancing. It really was big, Friday, Saturday and Sunday the dance hall was full, we didn't know how to dance so we would just stand by the door and watch all those young and middle-aged dancers, wishing we were dancing too. When it was time to go home we would stop at a little restaurant to eat. After a while we got to know a cute little waitress, she was the only one working every night, I noticed on her finger she had a wedding ring, I asked about her husband and she said she wasn't married so I asked why the ring? She said, 'If someone asks me to go out, I can say I am married.' If I liked someone, I would say the same thing I am telling you. So I said the next time I come in if I don't see the ring on your finger I will ask you to go out with me. A few days later, we went in and sure enough, the ring was not there, so I ups and ask for a date, she agreed. On the night of the date, I rented a yellow roadster and took her for a ride to places she told me because I didn't know the town. It was a nice evening, yes, I must have kissed her but no sex, and that was the only time that I took her out, I don't know why but that's the way it was. Later while visiting a dance hall one evening Willy found a ladies wristwatch and I talked him out of it and gave it to the waitress I had taken out, it was a nice watch with little diamonds around the face. Well more about that watch later.

We were working six days a week, you might wonder what we did on Sundays, well no kidding we could not do anything as we had to spend Sundays at the bosses house, the only one who didn't have to be there was the older truck driver because he was married, but the two brothers, Willy, Nat and I had to be there every Sunday all day. We were served a big meal and after we would sit and talk or watch the baseball game at the park. Let me say he did not compel you to be there but if you did not he would be offended, guess he was lonely because he had only girls to talk to. I will say it wasn't bad spending Sunday there, plenty to eat, all you want in fact; it was good and kind of him. Well this went on for quite a while, everything was going smooth, then one day he came up with a bright idea, he bought four Model T trucks and on slow days we were to go out and sell fruit door to door, two men to a truck. I had to get the trucks and drive them one by one to his home and park them on the empty lot next to his home. It was a job I didn't care for, as I never drove a Model T truck, but by driving slow, I got all the trucks to his home. Now by not going home after work we hung around town every night and began getting to bed late every night so it became hard for us to get up on time, Tuesday and Thursdays were the worst days for us, I don't know if the weather had anything to do with it or not, however being that Willy slept in the garage he was sent to wake us up when we overslept. I really didn't like being late, I even hung the alarm clock over our heads so we would wake up but to no avail, it didn't help. One Thursday we overslept, Willy came and woke us up we said okay but when he left we went back to sleep, Willy came again but by then it was really late. We got up raced to the house put the stalls on the truck, raced to the market loaded the fruit that had to go on, Raced to the storage house loaded the remainder of what had to be put on. Then we jumped in the truck and I was driving like hell to the market to set things up and as I turned the corner almost where we were to set up, I hit a low branch and knocked some grapefruits off the truck, buy this time our boss was standing on the street

looking our way. I stepped out of the truck and looked at him kind of sheepishly with a smile on my face, but he was just looking. Nat and I got busy gathering the grapefruits off the street and went to set up the stalls, I don't remember what he said but I am sure it wasn't too much as I said before he was a patient man. I remember something he would say if he saw a bad fruit on the stand while you were standing working the stand, he would say, while you're standing there like a flower pot get that bad fruit out and replace it. he never raised his voice. Nat would get a big kick out of that and laugh out loud. This brings something to mind, when I was young if I had a mishap I would look at it with a funny smile on my face, I don't know why I guess that was one of my many shortcomings. One day I was backing the Model T truck on the lot next to the boss's house, there was a small incline and the amount of gas I was giving the truck could not make the little incline, I was afraid to give it more gas for fear I would have a problem. The boss was with me; he said, give it more gas, I did and backed it into the other truck that was behind and right into the radiator. I got out with a smile on my face, he looked at me and said,

"I can see people making a mistake but I can't see someone making one and coming out with a smile about it."

Yes, I knew he was right but what could I do? I thought that by smiling he would not feel too bad about the accident. In a short while it was over and he wasn't angry, as I said before, he was a good man he had a way of seeing that things just happen and that was that. Things went on as usual, we worked in the store when it was busy, when they became slow we went out with the truck and sold fruit and vegetables house to house, I enjoyed working house to house, we were on our own and free. We always had a lot of fun, the days were always nice, except in the morning due to the fog, which lasted until around nine o'clock, then the sun would come out and it would be nice. Sometimes the boss would make a special sale on Saturdays, he would buy about thirty or forty lugs of seedless grapes and the brothers would make a stack about six feet high, then the boss would run an ad in the paper, 'special grapes 5 lbs., for 10 cents'. Boy that would draw a big crowd to the market and all the departments in the market would benefit. Saturdays were always our busiest day of the week. We would spend our lunch hour in the alley between the market and the next building, it was a large empty building except for a motorcycle, I didn't know who the owner was but every lunch time I would go in and look at it, I wanted to ride it but I didn't know how, I would turn it over in my mind what I needed to do if I got on it, well this went on within me for days, then one day Nat was with me and I decided to give it a try. I got on, started it, put it in gear and I was riding but now I was in trouble I couldn't stop it. I was confused where is?? What do I do?? What flashed into my mind was the episode riding the horse in Texas, I knew I came out good there because I didn't lose my head, but this was different, I seen the wall coming closer, I said to myself 'stupid you better do something quick or you're going to slam into the wall and lose your head!' So to avoid hitting the wall I lifted

108

my right leg up and made the cycle fall on its side. I hurt my leg a little because I didn't lift it quite high enough. Hobbling around I lifted the cycle and put it in its right place and saw the damaged was some scratches that made me feel bad. There wasn't any more cycle riding after that. Well another stupid thing done in my youth.

Weeks went by after that with just working, nothing else or anything different to do. Sometimes we would go down to the gambling ship never winning we didn't go there very often, instead we would go watch the dancers do their stuff like I said that was the craze in those days. Well the inevitable finally happened, we were fired and it was my fault. I will tell you why, for some time on those Tuesdays and Thursdays when we had to go to the market square to set up the booths, we also had to go to the store and pick up some fruit or whatever it was we had orders for. It was always very early in the morning before anyone was there, so I would go behind the lunch counter and make us malt shakes, this had been going on for several weeks and we kind of looked forward to it, well anyway we didn't know but someone was stealing groceries, Not on the same days we were there but the boss had someone in the store all night for several days to see who was stealing, so we were caught drinking malts and eating cookies. I tell you we never stole anything other than the cookies and malts, but that was wrong, anyway we were fired, well Nat and I, Willy was not fired. I think it was because Nat and I were from New York and the boss didn't know what to think of us, maybe he thought we were gangsters. He used to ask a lot of questions when he would let us take the truck home in the evenings. Things like, what do you do in the evening, so maybe it bothered him us being from New York, anyway being caught helping ourselves to malts and cookies was enough to get Nat and I fired, I suppose he figured we were stealing other stuff. I remember Nat and I looked at each other with a questionable expression, both thinking, what do we do now? When we got back to our place, we talked about what we should do next. I suggested, we buy a truck and peddle fruit. That is what we did; we bought a Model A Ford and moved to the city, in to a rooming house. Willy decided to move there too but he got his own room. Now we were businessmen or should I say business boys? On the first day of our new venture we got up early and set out to the market to buy apples and potatoes; these two items were always a pretty good seller at the store so we were sure we wouldn't have any trouble selling them. All went very well for a few days, we were able to make ends meet and it was a lot of fun for us. With that thought in mind, there we were in business for ourselves, but being young; we didn't do the right thing to begin with. On the days that were slow, we would sell our merchandise for what we paid for it, which was a big mistake as I am sure you can see. It didn't take us long to see our mistake because after buying our food, paying our rent etc., we didn't have anything left. Our thought was not to be left with stuff that we didn't sell so at least we would make our money back... well we realized that that kind of business would soon put us out of business. It was near the end of November I remember, and pretty cold in the mornings. I remember in order to start the truck, because of the cold we had to jack one of the rear wheels up which made it easier to crank the engine, in those days the Model T did not start easy in cold weather; so every morning we spent a half hour or so cursing, kicking tires and knocking on the hood until it started, like all that nonsense helped any, it was getting the best of us. By nine o'clock, the weather warmed up nicely but those mornings were cold and foggy.

Now the second episode with the wristwatch Willy had found. If you remember he gave it to me and I gave it to the girl from the restaurant I had taken out that one time. Well one day he come to me and asks for the watch back, I told him I didn't have it, I didn't tell him I gave it away. Anyway he didn't believe me and he gave me until the following Friday or Saturday, I don't remember which, until five-O'clock to produce it or else. I didn't know what his 'or else' meant; I told him I would be in my room if he wanted to talk to me. I had about three or four days to wait for whatever was to come. As I worked during the day selling fruit from house to house, I kept thinking about the deadline that was to come. I kept asking myself what will happen, I'd say to myself, maybe I was wrong for taking the wristwatch from him and giving it to the waitress, but then I'd think, well he gave it to me, why did he give it to me? Maybe because when he hung on to us when we met and through me he got a job and in appreciation he gave me the watch, if that's the case why would he want it back now. Anyway I kept thinking of this 'High Noon" at five O'clock. We would see him on another job as we passed going to work in the morning but not a word was spoken. Finally, the day comes, I went to work as usual, at the end of the day Nat and I came home and waited, as there was nothing else we could do until the episode passes one way or another. I remember looking at the clock, five on the dot, I was listening for his door to open and then a knock on our door, a few minutes after five and nothing. We wanted to go out and do something not sit there in suspense. Finally way after five I began to dress to go out, I had a faint idea that perhaps he was bluffing when he made the threat although I wasn't sure. As it turned out, I was right he didn't show up and I never heard anything about it again. Well that problem was solved but we had other problems to solve, we were going deeper in the hole every day because we were spending our money too fast and not charging enough, so we were running out of money to purchase more fruit and vegetables. I think you can guess what is coming, we ended up going out of business. So what now? Well we sold the truck and after a few days decided to go back East, back to the big city of New York, it was about four weeks before Christmas and I always wanted to be home on the holidays as that has always been the holiday I really love. Christmas always gave me a warm feeling and whenever I would sing Silent Night the tears were ready to come, but I held them back as much as possible. I didn't want anyone to see me cry. As I look back, I see I never would miss being home for Christmas if at all possible. After packing the things that we didn't want to carry with us, we sent them to my folks and we hit the road hitchhiking through Arizona, we slept in the local jails at night, remember I told you some towns would let you sleep in the jail when you were passing through. One night in jail we met a man who was on crutches, something was wrong with one of his legs. While having a conversation with him, he pulled out his spoon a match and some Opium and proceeded to heat the Opium put it in a syringe and shoot it in his vein. He asked if I wanted to give it a try. NO SIR! Was my reply, I didn't want any of that stuff that was one thing I was not eager to try. The odd thing about this man was how he was getting the money for his habit, he had a letter signed by some Governor in what state I can't remember, in the letter it stated, I am a cripple and have eight children and a wife, I can't work so I am trying to get enough money to buy a peanut stand. Let me explain about the peanut stand, It wasn't a stand that is in one place always, this is the kind of unit that was on wheels and was wheeled from place to place, I don't think any of you ever seen one, maybe in movies. Anyway, there were many of them around at that time. You should remember the monkey and the organ grinder, I am talking about the organ on wheels, the peanut unit was the same idea. You probably have seen an organ grinder and monkey in movies too. Well this guy was making money pretending he was begging for money for his family. The letter had to be a phony but in those days people were very considerate and always donated when they saw a cripple or blind man, maybe thinking he was a soldier from the first world war. I remember when I was young it amazed me how people would give to the needy especially soldiers. This guy bragged about how much money he was able to get with that letter.

The next morning we were let out and we hit the road again towards New Mexico, there isn't much to say about those little towns back then, sidewalks were mostly wood and covered with the extensions from the buildings, which was the only place a person could get away from the sun during the day. From what I recall the people were mostly Indian and Mexican, standing under those extensions in groups. We spent a night in their jail just to sleep, while in there one Mexican committed suicide during the night in another cell. In the morning the doors were opened and we were let out, it was always a relief to step out into the morning air, we never knew if we would be detained for questioning and we were always worried about that when we asked to be put up for the night.

Now to get on with my story, I must tell you that in all my travels going through many states I always felt that New Mexico was the most desolate. The towns were very small and far apart and it was so very, very hot, one could see the heat waves rise from the ground. You would think things would burn up in all that heat, yet somehow desert grasses grew along with sage brush and cactus, all survived the burning heat. The people took it in their stride having lived there for years, no wonder the skin on their faces tell of the beating it took from the

sun. When on the road, walking between the small towns there was nothing to see but sand with mountains in the background. For long periods of time there weren't any cars passing, it seemed like everything and everyone was wiped from the face of the earth and we were the only ones left. I remember thinking about being the only ones left on earth many times when we were in vast open spaces with nothing or no one in sight. Well, we weren't making much headway on the road so we decided to go to the nearest freight yard. When we found one there were quite a few young men waiting for the same thing, a freight train to hop. It was late I remember when we got to the yard and I hated hopping a train in the dark, but one can't be too choosey so we waited for the next train to be pulling out. Finally we heard the whistle, you know, the 'High Ball' we knew the train would be starting so we got ready, it's like ready, set, go, because you can't do anything until the train is moving. When I mentioned the whistle we heard, the 'high ball', I meant a train with that whistle had about 100 cars and must have been about a mile long. Then the sound came, the throbbing locomotive pulling the weight of all those cars, the wheels turning slowly at first then faster, we got ready to jump it. I had a second to look around and there were many guys running toward the train, naturally, it becomes a scramble, everyman for himself. I ran as fast as I could, grabbed on and pulled myself in the box car but lost Nat, so I climbed to the top of the train and kept walking from boxcar to boxcar, looking in the reefers calling his name but there was no answer. I did all this in the dark and I remember I was scared and had to be very careful, because you never knew what would come up ahead, a low bridge or I could stumble and fall. After a while I stopped looking for Nat and decided I had better look for a place to get out of the open. I found I could easily jump into another boxcar. I found one open and jumped in then I realized why it was left open... the car was full of onions. A young kid was already inside, we had to make the best of it, smelling onions all night, it was awful, we had to endure it also all the next day

as the train made no stops. The second night was coming up but we were still traveling, so there we were the onions and us. Sometime in the early morning hours the train pulled into a yard, but we sat tight and listened because sometimes a train would pull in and break up, leaving some cars and hook up others then be on its way again. So be sat and waited and yes it was breaking up, we could hear rumbling then all of a sudden our car was moving, we sat not saying a word wondering what was happening, as long as we were moving and we could hear the engine we felt we were alright. However, not the case this time, we stopped and continued standing still. I heard the engine was moving away which made me think we might have been put on a side track, so I climb up and stuck my head out the top vent to see what was going on, sure enough we were on the side track, meaning this car was there to stay. It was still dark outside and I turned and told the kid who was there with me that we better get out and go get on the freight train that was moving on. We scrambled out and ran for the rest of the moving

114

train. We made it by getting into another boxcar, which had other men already inside. I was hoping I could find my friend Nat, but no such luck. I made myself as comfortable as I could and tried to get some sleep. I tell you the ride was pretty rough, you keep bouncing up and down, no way to find a comfortable position, you sit, stand, lay down, but nothing really helps, you just have to make the best of it.

We rode most of that day and in the very late afternoon the train arrived at its destination. It no sooner came to a halt and a great many men got off. It seemed to me we were like locust invading and heading toward town with one idea, to get something to eat. As I was walking toward town, I keep wondering whatever happened to Nat? In front of me, about twenty yards away a bunch of men were walking in a group, I thought I spotted Nat, it made me feel good to see him because I was afraid that he might have been left behind. I called out his name and it was him, he stopped and I soon caught up with him, we couldn't figure out how we lost each other, but we were happy to be together again and the fear of losing each other didn't mean much anymore. We got to town, bought something to eat, found somewhere to sit and eat, we met and began talking with some of the men that were on the train also, men who knew the hitch-hiking score better than we did. They asked if we wanted to go to the hobo jungle, at that time there was one near this town. We said sure not knowing what a hobo jungle was but it was something new and interesting to us at the time. We found out people who travel the rails most of the time know about these places, 'Hobo Jungles'. Whoever goes there, if they have food they give what they have, if it needed to be cooked, it was cooked. Cooked or ready to eat all would be gathered and shared to all, whether you gave or not. These places were in the open and you would always find people there. If you stay all night you slept on the ground, although not all towns would tolerate a Hobo Jungle. We had heard of other places such as this but we never went to any of them. This was our first visit to one and I must say it was a nice experience, I don't recall if we slept there or not but all in all it was a nice experience, one would be afraid to go to a place like that now, probably it would be full of sick, mentally ill addicts of one kind or another, but in those days so many regular people were just out of work and had nowhere else to go. From here on, the trip back home is very vague; I tried very hard to remember but no luck.

We arrived at my folks home a few days before Christmas, the family was happy to see me, like I said before, whenever I left on one of my trips my folks never heard from me until they seen my face. I know it was wrong, seems when one is young one is sometimes inconsiderate of the ones left behind, especially mom's and dad's. The main thing was I had come home in good health but broke, and when one is in that condition where else would one go? That is the place you know a meal is always waiting for you and there is nothing like spending that one special day, Christmas at home with mom and dad, sisters and brothers. On this return, I think we stayed a little too long, I think it must have been about three weeks; finally, my mother gave me the hint to get to work. I remember I got a little angry, I knew she was right, after all if I was the only one there maybe she would not mind but Nat was there too and it cost money to feed two young healthy men. So there was nothing left to do but get our things together and head for the big city once again.

Well back in New York we tried to get work at the same outfit that once employed us but no openings this time around, so we took some temporary work in the city itself. We again met Tony, he had a job in a nice place and while working there, he met a girl cashier and they were going out pretty steady, he kind of fell for her. On his days off, he would take her out or go to her folk's house for dinner, so he was too busy to bother much with us. I also met the Jewish fellow that was our partner in the car deal for our trip, the car we sold in Arizona, remember? He asked for his money back but I told him, sorry you backed out at the last minute from going with us on that trip, we feel we don't owe you any money. That didn't satisfy him at the time, however after that, I heard no more about the money.

After working a while at this and that we got a call from the place we wanted to work again, Nat and I were hired to work in another of the owner's restaurants, this one was on 182nd Street and Broadway, it was near the George Washington bridge so we moved to 72nd Street near Lexington Ave. We found a nice big room on the third floor front; really, it was two rooms, a large living room and a bedroom with two beds. Tony moved in with us. This rooming house had man and women, this was the first time while in New York that we found a rooming house that rented to both sexes, I must say once again this was the best rooms we ever had, two big windows in the front room overlooking the street and it felt homey. We liked it very much so that's where we lived, Traveling every day to 182nd to work, we went by express subway so it didn't take too long.

Nat and I were both counter men at work, the manager took a liking to Nat and it was not long he made him a waiter, that gave Nat a chance to make more money, I have to admit it made me a little jealous because everybody that works in a restaurant always wants to be a waiter I never made it, I guess no one liked me or thought I would be a good waiter. Nat turned out to be a very good waiter, he had a nice disposition, I might add here that all the time we spent together we never had an argument, never even a harsh word, we always got along and were very good friends. I always liked him very much, I can't say the same thing about Tony, we did get into it once in a while. I must admit many times it was my fault, but he would sometimes give me a little too much lip and then we were at it. I better get back to my story, we didn't know anybody in the rooming house up to this point, but we soon did. One evening it was about ten o'clock, we were coming home and as we opened the front door, we heard loud voices, an argument. We reached the second floor and there we stopped, being nosey, we wanted to know what all the commotion was about. There were two girls standing there, so you might say that was reason enough to stop, one girl was in her nightgown, and the couple that were arguing were going down the stairs still going at it, I was leaning against the railing with my hand on the post which was round on the top, this girl in the nightgown leaned over the post to look down, as she did her breast nipple fell between my finger, and naturally I pinched it, but to my surprise she didn't even flinch, I expected a slap in the face but nothing happen, and that was the beginning of our friendship. She was a divorcee; her name was Kitty Kelly, and a good looker. Yes, you guessed it she was Irish, she had dirty blond hair, very pretty, I really liked her at the time, and we became close friends, whenever she would go out I would wait up for her, I remember one night she went out, I think it was to a party and she had too much to drink, she had no one to bring her home and was afraid to stay there so she called me and had me come get her and bring her home. I guess she didn't trust staying overnight where she was. I brought her home and put her to bed, she was drunk, I can't say that she was very drunk just wobbly on her feet. After I put her in bed thinking she might get sick during the night I was looking for something to put by the bed in case she got sick, I couldn't find anything. The nearest thing that came to mind was a dish from under a flowerpot and I took a glass shade from an electric light bulb that was on the wall. I put the shade upside down on the dish and put it by her bed and left. The next day she told me when she awoke and saw the dish there and figured out why I put it there she laughed. I, myself thought it was silly because if she got sick that would not hold anything, anyway that was the best I could do at the time. I know what you're thinking but you're wrong I didn't have sex with her. Oh, I know I could have I'm sure, but the truth is I didn't, why, I can't really explain, maybe my upbringing.

At the restaurant about that time Nat met and got to talking to a customer who said, he could get us a job on a ship going to France. That was one place we really wanted to go. We wanted to see Paris and other parts of Europe, to travel across the big ocean, to be a seaman, we both liked the idea. If we could succeed in getting that job it would fulfill our dreams, mine especially. In my early days in New York as I said earlier in this story, I went many times to the docks and watch ships come and go, I would stand there and dream of going with the ship as it departed. Now here was the chance to do just that, my dream just may come true. We started preparing for the trip, the fellow was to tell us when everything was ready, which ship we would travel on and so forth. Every time he came into the restaurant, we would ask when we would be going. The answer was always not yet. Therefore, we just waited and hoped. Then finally he came in and told us we were to leave the following week, so again we tell the manager we will be leaving, I think that week was the longest week I ever had, the day before we were to leave

we told the land lady that we defiantly would not need the room anymore, we packed our things in a suit case and met the fellow by the dock near where the ship was docked. The name to the ship was the Majestic. We arrived by taxi, met the fellow and the first thing he said was where is the money. We were taken aback because there was no mention of money ever before. We didn't understand what he meant, and then he said, how did you think I was going to get you a job on the ship? Well I'll tell you if he would have asked us for a dollar he could not get it because we were flat broke, that was it, he got kind of mad and went away leaving us there. It took us a while to figure this guy out, he was a con man because he didn't bring us on the ship he wanted the money about a block from the gangplank. If we would have given him the money by the time we got on the ship he would have been long gone, and we would have boarded the ship, ending up looking like fools because no one would have known anything about any jobs. Of course we never saw the guy again, and yes we did get our jobs back and the same room because Tony was staying behind, he had that girl and he didn't want to go anywhere. YES! We were very disappointed, for me it was a dream that was shattered, because that was the one chance I felt I had to see Europe and it turned out to be a con-man we were dealing with. At that time we were not wise to the ways of the world, we were innocent small town bumpkins. Anyway, as it turned out time heals all disappointments and I soon forgot about it at least that was what I was trying to make myself believe at the time. Therefore, to drown my sorrow I would go to a speakeasy after work with the waiters and drink needle beer.

(Web- Definition of NEEDLE BEER: beer made with ether alcohol often illicitly and under makeshift conditions. For a big depression buck, you could get ten glasses of needle beer.)

I don't know why they called those places Speakeasy's, my thought is that after they let you in, first seeing who you were through a peep hole in the door, you were told not to talk too loudly for fear the police might hear the gathering and raid the place. Anyway, the beer did taste good and I enjoyed it. It made one feel like (what the hell lets have another) and another until your legs were wobbly then you were ready to go home.

From here on my story is broken because I can't recall why we left where we were working and found ourselves working in Woodside, for the same company. That was Woodside Long Island, and there again I was the Spaghetti cook and Nat was a counter man. Tony was still in New York; still with the same girl and from what I gathered at the time he was pretty serious about her. I'm sure he would have married her if she would say the word. Nat and I rented a room in a private home, our room was right off the living room. The home was owned by a French couple and they lived in the house, no children, the house was kept very clean and the owners were in their middle thirties or there about. There are two things I remember about living there, one is I found out after I married your mother that her sister Josie and her sisters husband Fred were visiting those people while Nat and I were living there. I remember seeing people there sometimes on Sunday evenings when we returned from work. Of course at the time I didn't know it was your mother's sister; and she always wanted to bring your mother to meet us. However, that never happen, now whether she wanted to get your mother to meet Nat or myself I don't know. I say that because Nat was a good looking fellow, more so then me, anyway that was what I thought at that time, I suppose that may be the reason I never found a girl to go out with me, I'm talking about in my home town years. Now the other thing I often think about is what happened in the place where I was working. This place was in a section where the business was pretty slow, I wondered why they ever opened a restaurant there, but it was there and I had a job so why worry. Well anyway in May came a holiday, Memorial Day, the cemetery was just a few blocks walking distance from the restaurant, I came to work that day thinking this will be a slow day because everyone was home, and if they go to the cemetery to visit their loved ones, who would be hungry if sorrow sets in. Well lo and behold they started to come from all directions. I thought the dead were also coming in, that was the busiest day I put in, in all the years I worked and in all the restaurants I ever worked. I cooked ten boxes of spaghetti, there were twenty-one pounds in each box and a serving per costumer was one quarter of a pound. You do the math. That night I went to bed early, and slept like a log. We didn't work there very long because the place was going to close. Happily, we were offered a job in Jamaica Long Island we took it. On the last night, we packed our things and sneaked out the window, the reason was we were behind in our rent, not a very nice thing to do. Well that closes the chapter of living in Woodside, Long Island.

When we moved to Jamaica, Long Island Tony moved in with us. There were two places I did not care to work, one was on Broadway in New York, I mentioned it earlier in my story, and the second one was in Jamaica. Don't ask me why I couldn't give you a proper reason, I guess

I didn't know why myself, but as before a job is a job and I needed one.

Not far from where we were working, there was a park, and many times Tony and I would walk through there, sometimes sit on one of the benches and talk or just plain dream. Well on one of those, evenings in the park we saw this beautiful girl sitting alone, so we stopped and struck up a conversation. It was hard at first but we did not give up. Finally, we got her to respond. After talking we found out that her sister Inez was with her. Inez had a date with her boyfriend, Harold he was working as an usher in a theater nearby and your mother was to meet his friend, it was a blind date for your mother. After talking for a while we asked her to walk with us until the movie ended and she was to meet Inez, Harold and the blind date. By that time, I was telling Tony to take a walk and he was telling me the same thing, so neither of us left. She was too pretty to leave and the time flew by and we missed her sister Inez and the blind date. Now what to do, she did not want to go home without her sister, you see Inez was younger and your mother was to look after her. Well it was getting rather late, past midnight and no sign of Inez. So we took your mother home which wasn't far from the park, although we had to take a streetcar, we didn't know what to expect when we got her home our only wish was that Inez was home and safe. When we arrived there and explained what happen, to her folks we left, but on the way to her home I had asked her for a date, she did consent but stood me up, so on my next day off Tony and I went to where she lived and waited for her to come home from work. She had told us she worked at Macy's warehouse but I had no idea when she would be coming home, I just waited, I was determined to see her again. There was a firehouse on one of the corners by her house and that is where we stood, watching every direction not to miss her. Finally we seen her, Jane Mansfield had nothing on your mother as far as figures go. She seen me and I walked over to her, we talked and before I left I had another date, this time her sister was coming along with her boyfriend, I was glad she said yes. That left poor Tony out in the cold.

I was now seeing your mother every week or more often. At first her folks thought I was, a gangster because I was always dressed very well with a flower in my lapel, gloves in hand and spats. I don't remember exactly the time of year we met but I am sure it was winter or early spring because I was wearing my winter topcoat. I think it was in the early part of the year. Why am I saying this is because in the following summer I went to work in New Jersey at a recreation park, it was Palisade Park, I was doing nothing but making and dishing out coffee; it kept me plenty busy. The reason so much coffee was being sold was because there was a swimming pool and loads of people were in and out of the pool and every time they came out, they would buy coffee to warm up. I would see your mother every week one way or the other and during the week I would write to her. Once or twice she came up to the park with Inez and spent some time with me and after I got off I would take her home. I worked there all summer. That September we were married. Therefore, the third stage of my life began, and that is another story.

To say a few words about my friends Nat and Tony before I begin the third part of this my life. After I was married they came and visited us and gave us a mantle clock for a wedding present, I don't know where the clock is now. I saw Nat once more after that in New York he was a shoe salesman in a shoe store, about Tony, as I told you in the early part of my story he had something the matter with him as far as his health. A few years into my marriage I found out that he went back home and passed away at a young age, I have thought of them so many times throughout my life, the three of us were so very close and did so much together those few years of our youth.

Here I will close the second part of my young life.

CIRCA 1932 - 1947
Marriage and Children

This is the third part of my story, life together with your mother, from our wedding day until the time we as a family moved to California, so when I say I did this or did that, you must know it includes your mother. However, before I start I will back up a little. Before I met your mother I was attending a school, I wanted to be one of 'The Ten Thousand Finest in New York', a police officer. At that time, New York had ten thousand police officers and that is what they were called, the ten-thousand finest. The school was called Delancey School, I attended it three nights a week, but after your mother and I were married I had to give it up as you will see as my story progresses.

We met in very early spring and were married in September, September 19th 1931 to be exact. The wedding day was on a Saturday afternoon, your mother lived at 168th Street the church was only half a block away on Parson Blvd, a Catholic church. It was a double wedding; her sister Inez and Harold were married with us. Her folks made all the arrangements, my father, mother, sisters and brother all came from Jersey to attend. The best man was a friend of the family, his name was John Maugerri, the g is pronounced like a J, and he paid for the ceremony at the church. It's funny how money talks, Harold and Inez had to be married in the rectory because Harold was not catholic. Your mother and I were married at the Altar. I remember the priest was behaving sort of abrupt, I wondered what was wrong. Soon the priest went into the rectory and John went after him and when they came back the priest was brushing John's coat, I knew then that John must have given him money because all was fine after that. I recall that incident many times and say to myself even in the house of God money talks.

The wedding in the church went off just fine, the reception was at your mother's parent's home all the food was prepared, it was a help yourself affair, lots of Italian goodies and plenty wine to drink. There also was music for dancing, I cannot remember who or what was played and toward the evening the firemen from the firehouse came over some with instruments and played. Your uncle Fred got a washtub from somewhere and they followed one another around the house with Fred playing the metal washtub. What a racket but everyone was enjoying themselves. It was a day not to be forgotten and as you see, I never forgot it. The evening ended about eleven o'clock and we were to leave on a week's honeymoon to Atlantic City. We were to sleep one night in New York, I had collected eighty dollars from my family, Harold, did not get any money so I had to pay for everything until we got back then he would pay me back, which he did. In those days eighty dollars was a lot of money so I had enough.

After saying goodbye to all we were driven to a bus station, the bus took us to New York and we spent the night in the Alexander Hotel, it wasn't far from Times Square. The next morning we were on our way to Atlantic City by bus, it wasn't far from New York and didn't take long to get there. You might ask, why Atlantic City, why not Coney Island? Coney Island is right in New York and a very nice place. I can answer that easily, as long as I lived in New York I only went to Coney Island once. With ten million people in New York and on a hot weekend between one and two million people go to the beach at Coney Island, just imagine all those people on the beach you couldn't see any sand just people. Beside with all those people it ends up standing room only, and if you go for food or a drink, you can't find you place anymore, like a carpet of humanity. People would put up a stick with a flag on it so they could find their way back but after a while there were so many flags, they were lost again. Too many flags and too many colors, so you see why we chose Atlantic City, besides it was the city for honeymooners. It was smaller than Coney Island and a lot nicer. Let me say that people with money went there to spend their vacations. After we arrived, we checked into a hotel for a one-week stay, the name of that hotel I'm not sure but the name that keeps coming to my mind is the Washington House. To us at that time it was a very nice place; it reminded me of being on a ship. The halls were about six feet wide, red carpet with a little design, all the wood was painted white, the walls had wallpaper on them, can't recall the color. It had a warm feeling every time you would walk in.

I think we got there some time after four o'clock, and after unpacking; we must have gone out for something to eat. Being it was September and daylight savings time we walked around the pier for quite a while then returned to the hotel. You know how honeymooners are they spend a good deal of time in the hotel room. Well we didn't spend all our time there, we would go out to eat, take in the sights, walk on the pier, it was a very long pier and the breeze coming from the ocean was enjoyable for all of us I remember. We took pictures on the walks they are in the family album. Our room connected with Harold and Inez's and we were in each other's room sometimes, I did spoil one evening for your mother, I asked her something and she gave me an answer in a kidding way and I took it wrong and walked out to take a walk and while walking I came to a theatre and went in to see the movie, the picture playing was titled 'The Bad Girl', funny I should remember that. After the movie I returned to the hotel, told your mother I was sorry but I knew I had hurt her a lot. I've thought of it many times and feel really sorry for what I did, Oh, I know there were many things that I did that hurt her during our married life, but it was on our honeymoon and that was so wrong. However we did enjoy our honeymoon very much, the walks, eating out, we even took in a few picture shows and walked on the beach near the water, of course always knowing that when the week ended it was back to work and at that time I was out of a job but I knew I wouldn't have any problem getting one if I went back to the restaurant, but I wanted to try something else.

So after a week of enjoying our honeymoon, which only came once in your mother and my life time we packed our things and took a bus and headed for Times Square, while we were on the bus we talked about our week trying to relive it, holding each other's hand feeling confident that the future will be good for both of us. Like I said before, the bus trip was a short one so before we knew it we were in New York. Oh, I know we all wished that we could have ridden that bus forever but no we had to face reality, it was back to work. When we reached New York and got off the bus we didn't stop at Time Square to walk around as it was after noon and we had a distance to go before reaching home. We got on a subway heading for Jamaica and that was quite a long ride, all the way to the end of the line. After reaching the end, we had to take a streetcar to bring us home. When I say home I mean your mother's parent's

home, we had to stay with them for a while. The house had three bedrooms, a pretty good size kitchen, a large dining room, living room and a sun porch. Your mother and I were given the front bedroom, Inez and Harold preferred to live in the attic, I guess they wanted all the privacy they could get, it was a large attic and they were happy having it. We paid eighteen dollars a week, which was a lot of money for us to pay but we had no alternative, as you will understand later on. As soon as we were settled in, I spent the next few days trying to decide where to go to find a job. I didn't care to go to the restaurant because I would most likely have to work Sundays and your Mother and I didn't want that, although at the time it was depression and jobs were not easy to get unless you knew someone, then you could usually find work.

I will try to explain how things were then. During those days, the Democratic Party had control of New York, it was known as the Tammany Hall.

128

Web: (Tammany Hall, also known as the Society of St. Tammany, the Sons of St. Tammany, or the Columbian Order, which was a New York City political organization)

The city was divided into sections and each section had an alderman, this is the man you had to see if you wanted a job, but to see him you had to be sent to him by someone who had a direct pull with him. After finding someone that had authority, I went to see the man. One thing, you had to be a democrat or no job. Well I needed a job so I was a democrat with all my heart and whatever else need be. He sent me to a bus company, the name of the bus company was North Shore Bus Co., and I was hired with three other young fellows. They proceeded to teach us how to drive a bus, that took about two weeks, then we went down for uniforms that were made to our measurements, the color was a blue-gray, the style was like that of the California motorcycle cops with the high boots. Only we didn't have the boots we had what were called at the time leggings, they fit over the top of the shoes and the lower part of the pants, I tell you with that uniform on we looked like Gestapo's. Well I was now a bus driver and the hours were crazy, split shift, Sunday's too. I had to get up at 5 am, but it was a job. I soon discovered that working at a job that was gotten through a political party you were exposed to a large amount of abuse by the company. First the superintendent held all the power, he wanted every employee to know your life depended on him and I had a feeling he didn't care much for me. I soon could see that he liked choosing a few fellows to pick on to show all, he was boss. I knew from the beginning that the job would be limited, not that I wouldn't do my very best but even if you were the best, you still would not be good enough for him, so I kept a low profile as they say. When I saw him first I made sure I was facing the other way, I just wanted to stay out of his way, I didn't want anything to happen to lose my job, after all I just starting working there. I remember on one occasion I was sitting in the bus at the station waiting for the people to get on, at that time we were getting sixty cents an hour and I was thinking, gee that's a lot of money, sixty cents, that's a penny a minute, at the restaurant you worked twelve hours a day six days a week for little more than I was making here with a lot less hours. Although driving bus I was only bringing home clear $18.00 a week and that was what we were paying a week for rent. That left us zero, not even enough to go to the movies on our day off, but I kept on working and watching my step making sure I did well, but things happen. Once I had a little accident, not much total damage, maybe fifty dollars and of course, it went against my record. Another time with about fifty people in the bus, early in the morning, people going to work, I was heading for the station going pretty fast, at times you had to speed up a bit so as not to get behind time. Every trip had a time limit and if you got behind time, it was difficult to catch up and of course, people don't want to be late for work. Well as I was coming down a little hill and with the bus full, some passengers standing I saw not far in front of the bus two little children started running across the street with a big dog behind them. I knew I couldn't come to a screeching stop because if I do all those people standing will fall towards the front of the bus, so I hit the brake a little but had to keep going no matter what. Thank God the two children made it across but the dog froze in his tracks and there he stood looking at me, yes I felt it when I hit him, I'll never forget it completely. When I pulled into the station, I could not go on, not because I killed the dog but the thought of suppose the kids froze and I killed them. I was really shaken up and scared, hence another mark on my record. Well, one has to keep going and I didn't give up the job, even with wondering at the time what may happen next, I was happy doing what I was doing, the money was no good and the hours always different but it was a job. I remember getting an all-day run to the end of the line, all the way to Flushing Bay, not that you would know where that was but it was some distance. Anyway it was a Saturday, a nice bright morning; however, about noon the wind started to blow and it became stronger by the hour. I remember I was standing waiting for the passengers or for my time to leave and I was watching a blimp in the sky, trying to make a landing but the wind was too strong, the blimp was having trouble and all of a sudden it was breaking up. It wasn't a passenger blimp, so not many people were on board. I could see the canvas ripping and two people falling out. This was happening over the lake and in a few moments, the whole thing fell into the lake. I know some were killed but how many I don't remember. I wanted to holler out, look everybody look what is happening, the people are falling, the thing is coming apart, but there was no one there but me at that moment. I remember wondering if I was the only one witnessing such a disaster. To see people falling from such a height, it is hard to explain what one feels in those moments. I guess sorrow and helplessness is what I felt. Then after seeing such a thing one had to go on like nothing happened, people started coming to the bus, getting in and it was like nothing happened at all they didn't see what happen they were just off to work. Again I have gotten away from my story well no that is part of my story, right?

I am working but not getting ahead financially. On my day off your mother and I sometimes would go out with her father for a ride, or buy groceries or go to the bakery down by the factory where her father and mother worked, they were both cigar makers, they were employed for the De Nobili Cigar Company, it was owned by a Mr. De Nobili, who lived in Italy.

Web: (De Nobili cigars are produced in Scranton, Pennsylvania, USA. Originating in 1896)

Your mother's parents were paid so much for every hundred made and they earned good money, also worked as many hours as they wanted. I don't mean more than eight hours; I mean any amount less than eight hours. It was a good job and no one seemed to ever get fired. All the employees were Italian, don't know if you had to be Italian but I don't think so. It was a job you could keep as long as you wanted it, sort of a craft thing; you had to be a good cigar maker. Anyway sometimes your mother and I would go out with her parents, as I said and we would go visit John the best man at our wedding. He was married and had two children, a boy and a girl. His wife worked too so his mother lived with them to take care of the children. From what I gathered, he was in the bootleg business, always going somewhere. One time he took me on his trip, but I sat in the car most of the time, he was in and out of the bars, what he was doing I had no idea but while sitting in the car people were going in and out of these bars and always looking at the car that I was in. I wondered why. You will find out why later on in the story. By this time your mother was in a family way with Rose, Inez was also in the same condition with your cousin Charlie. He was born two weeks before Rose.

I cannot recall exactly when, but soon after Rose was born I lost my job, that man with the power and the string he had me hanging on, was cut. So here I was no work, what to do now. Harold, Inez's husband was selling Wax Paper, door to door and making out. So that was what I became a door-to-door wax paper salesman. A package cost us $5.00, we would put fifteen sheets in an envelope and charge 15 cents, we were earning five dollars a day that was pretty good money those days. It sure was better than eighteen dollars a week at the bus company. After a while I would buy some paper napkins and sell them too, later on I sold the wax paper at two envelopes for 25 cents and with the napkins, I was still making a good living and I would get home early. Yet I remember if I had a choice between the two jobs I would have picked the bus driving. Oh, I know you may wonder why since I was making more money selling, and that was true but the bus driver job was more prestigious in my mind as a young man, it had its faults, less money etc., but I enjoyed the job. However, being married with a child on the way money was the prime concern and it was the worse depression in the history of the country, so if one had a job where he made pretty good money he was lucky. As I said it was the depression, you were all born into the depression but of course too young to realize the impact it had on our lives as a family. I remember the apple industry wanted someone to come up with an idea to promote the sale of apples; the prize for the winning idea was fifty dollars. Sure enough someone came up with the idea of people who were out of work purchasing a box of apples and standing on street corners or in front of high rise office building selling apples for ten cents each, not that the apples were worth that much but it was like a donation to the person and you received an apple in return. Just imagine standing on a corner in ten above zero or less and holding an apple in your hand waiting for someone to buy it. It was rough so my selling job may have been no picnic but it wasn't like that and I made a pretty good living at it for depression times. Keep in mind I am trying to sell fifteen sheets of wax paper for fifteen cents, that is a penny a sheet; you'd have to feel pretty sorry for the salesman to by those fifteen sheets. How many doors did I have slammed in my face, you can imagine, no wonder I preferred the bus drivers job. Harold and I were not the only ones trying to make a living door to door, I had people slam the door in my face, hide behind the curtains and not answer the door, they'd stand behind the curtain and watch me, sometime just for the hell of it I would keep ringing and make them come to the door, and sometimes I would just smile to myself and leave. I have to say sometimes it was so discouraging that I would get angry inside but I kept on going to one door after another. In the summer time, it was not bad but in the winter, I could not go out with a hat and coat on, to keep warm, if I did, I would not sell a thing. I had to give them the impression that I was really down and out, in a sense I had to play the part, I didn't like to do that but I had to sell. I had people give me hats and overcoats but I did not like it because I knew that when I would get around the corner I had to take it off and stuff it in the suit case where I kept the wax paper. I ended up with many overcoats and hats. Your mother's father would take them down to the poor section and give them away to people in need. At times, I had two over coats stuffed in the suitcase, no room for my wax paper; I had no choice but to do it that way. I feel better that the things went to the needy. I remember one time a lady gave me a hat and I put it on and a few days later, I had lice in my hair. I had to wash my head with kerosene; looking back at these things, I would say the majority of the people were kind and sympathetic. At the end I did not mind having the doors slammed in my face, I would just laugh and go on to the next house; you get hard after a while when you have to earn a living. I need to mention that your mother was still working at Macy's all this time, making drapes and curtains and taking them to customers' homes, she made pretty good money too. She was very good at her work as I am sure you remember with the fine clothing she made for all of us. Remember the western outfits she made for her and me to go square dancing in and the cowboy shirts she made for you and Sonny?

At this time the house where we were all was living had cesspool trouble. In those days there was no such thing as a septic tank, just a hole in the ground with rock piled up against the dirt so it didn't fall in, that was all that was required. Being that the first hole was too small to hold all the water, because now the family was larger, we decided to dig a new hole and make it bigger and deeper. We worked on Sundays and during the week too, instead of going out to sell wax paper, your mother's father would ask me to stay home and help. Your mother and I liked that because we would be together, and her father would charge us less rent that week. The job went on for weeks, at times her father, I guess I should call him your grandfather, even though all of you were not born yet, in fact, he would pass away when you mother was pregnant with Sonny.

Well back to the story, your mother's father would have two friends of his come over and help, they were regular ditch diggers and worked well; we finally dug down 22 feet and struck water at sea level that makes it a good cesspool when you reach water they never fill up. After finishing the cesspool it was back to the same thing, selling, and occasionally

134

going to the movies. Outside of that, we didn't do much of anything because your mother was getting big with Rose and the time was getting close. Inez was expecting any day now, the folks, were due to go on a vacation but grandma would not leave until Inez gave birth, which she did the later part of June, a son, your cousin Charlie was born. After everything was all right the folks left, I thought it strange that they didn't worry about their other daughter, your mother, who was due the early part of July. Well two weeks later Rose was born, no mother and no father for your mother, just Harold, Inez, myself and the doctor drinking coffee while waiting. Rose was born in the morning sometime between eight am and eleven am. Everything went fine. The doctors' name was Dr. Miole. Your mother developed an infection in her bladder, so the nurse would come over and take care of her. The nurse was the doctor's wife and he would come by to pick her up, doing this, he would charge us as a visit from him too. When the time came to pay him we paid what we thought was right

and that was all we paid. He never pressed for the rest.

With a baby we now had a lot of work to do, washing diapers every day and that was my job and I must say it was a nasty job. We didn't get to do much for enjoyment; we would take the baby out in the carriage and walk up and down the street. However, it was an enjoyment just to do that in those days because times were really rough not only for us but for everyone, we looked forward to our walks.

Now, to tell you a little about our neighborhood, if you walked to the front window and look out you would have seen that we only had one house to the right, a middle age couple lived there, they had two children, I should not have said children, as they were grownups. The girl was working and the boy was going to college. To the right of us there was a chain link fence and a large open field, on that field a large General Hospital was being built, a very nice looking building and it faced 160th Street. That was where the streetcar ran from Jamaica to Flushing. That is the streetcar I took to go to work at the bus company. To the left there were just two homes and an open field, the field we crossed when going to church on Sundays. Across the street were about four more homes and an open lot, and on the corner was the Fire Station, those were the firemen who made a lot of noise at our wedding. Diagonally across from our house lived a family, their name was Perezoni, they had two young children, and I think he was a schoolteacher. Your mother's family was friendlier with that family than any other on the street, the reason was that Mr. Perezoni had been giving piano lessons to Josie before she got married and moved out; he also gave lessons to Inez. However after she was married, he did not think it was his obligation anymore and Harold could not afford it, so she stopped taking lessons. But they still dropped in once in a while, the wife could never pronounce the letter V, she would pronounce it like a W, every time she would say elevator the V was a W and it struck me funny. I don't know why but it did. I do hope you get a pretty good picture of the area we lived in, lots of open space, if only a fellow had bought up some of it then, he would have become a millionaire. Oh, I must mention the house on the right of us was struck by lightning one stormy night. It struck the chimney and went all the way down to the cellar, it damaged the chimney a bit but that was all.

All the while we were living there your mother was after me to move us to our own apartment, she was always pressing the issue but I couldn't see it, keep in mind I had always been working in a restaurant before we married and my meals were always there, and now they were here together with her folks, I was a bit leery to go out on our own as we didn't make much money between us and now with a baby, we would talk about it in front of her father and he would never encourage the move. I would point that out to her and she would say maybe he doesn't want to lose the eighteen dollars a week we give him. Stupid me I couldn't see that, so we stayed and things were happening, her mother always wanted a country place, they were working toward changing the house for a country place in Pennsylvania, and when they did we were asked if we would like to move there too. Yes, we jumped at the chance, living in the country we thought would be wonderful. We moved in the fall it was a fourteen room house with eighty acres, some wood, some open range, lots of apple trees, one pear tree, a great big barn and a spring for drinking water which was brought to the house by gravity, it would run into a concrete tank and from there to the house. In the summer when rain was scarce the spring would flow slow so we had to watch how we used the water, but near the house we had a very large concrete tank that would catch the rain water from the roof, that water we used in the bath rooms, to wash the floors and wash clothes. We also had our own generator to make electricity, every day we would charge the batteries, and it worked out fine for lighting but we had to be careful we could not have a radio because the output was not high enough. The house itself was set on a hill so we had a nice view; it had a large front porch, which also ran down one side. The house itself was very nice, originally it had been used as a boarding house, a summer place for vacationers, that is why so many rooms. Inside there was a very large kitchen, a dining room where the help ate with a bedroom close by for the help. There also was a very large dining room for the guests; a large living room and all the bedrooms were upstairs. There was only one bathroom and that was downstairs, and no running water upstairs. The guests had a pitcher full of water and a basin to wash up in and a pot to do their duty in at night the alternative being to come down stairs or go out to the outhouse. All the furniture in the house were antiques, marble tops on the dressers, some of the beds were mahogany and some were brass, I am telling you real antiques. Nevertheless, all this was lost, as you will learn later.

The house was painted white with green trim, it was built up against a hill and the road ran in front of it, like all country roads it was dirt. As soon as it passed the house, it made a left turn and went right up the hill to woods. The big barn was across the road just a little to the right. It was a very old barn, no nails on the inside, all drilled and doweled. All the animal stalls were still intact, but the whole barn needed a lot of work. All the while we were there nothing was ever done to put it in better shape; I don't know why your mother's father didn't want to improve it. Mom and I loved living there, with eighty acres to roam, and that was what we did. Oh, we really enjoyed ourselves. After about a month of living there and getting set up I had to go into Stroudsburg PA, about eighteen miles away to apply for relief, in those days there wasn't any welfare or assistance it was known as relief. Your mom and I didn't have a car so Papa had to bring me. When I say Papa you will know that I mean your mother's father, probably don't need to say that but there it is. Well they allowed us a big four dollars a week for the three of us to live on, your mom, me and baby Rose that was it and no work to earn more. I'm sure the relief thought we had canned food to tide us over but of course being we just moved in we hadn't

any food except what we brought with us. I bought milk for Rose, although milk was only about ten cents a quart if I remember correctly, I bought it from a local farmer. I also bought chop meat or stew meat once a week and that was served on Sundays only, most of the time we had French fries with catsup. We accepted things as they were and never felt sorry for ourselves, we were young and we had each other. There were harder time though, I remember when I needed a pair of gloves to handle the wood in the winter snow, and a time when I needed a pair of overalls and had no money, I went to the general store in Tannersville and stole them, yes, I know what you're thinking and I make no excuse other than those days were rough, especially when you're in a strange state. With Pennsylvania Dutch, all around I had to fight or do twice as much work as the native to prove myself, as you will learn later on in the story.

Now to tell you a bit about the neighbors living close by. The nearest families to us were the Butz's, Mr. Butz and his wife and their four children, plus a grandchild of a daughter who never married. He had low blood pressure and to stay healthy he had to keep working, and that man did work. They had sixty acres and he tilled them all. He grew oats, buckwheat, corn and wheat. Some of the crop he would sell but most he raised for his livestock, Cows, chickens, pigs and horses to work the fields. He got laid up a couple times from horses kicking him once in the leg and once in the ribs. He was a tall man a little over six feet, big hands, just a big fellow all around. The next neighbor from him was a very short distance, his name was Dyson, he was an elderly man and his wife passed away before we moved there and he didn't do much farming, a couple cows was about all he had. The place was un-kept and overcome by weeds. But what could one old man do? Further down the road from his farm lived a family by the name of Tucker, they also were old people, they had two sons, and I knew the younger son best his name was Jim. A little further still from the Tucker's lived an Italian man his wife was not Italian, she was his second wife, they had two girls one about fifteen years old the other about five. He didn't own the place; a Jewish family from New York owned it. There were two homes on the property, the Italian fellow and his family lived in one and the Jewish family occupied the larger one when they came down for weekends and vacations. These are the four families that we knew more than any other, although Mrs. Tucker had a sister living close by and we visited her once or twice, also Mr. Dyson had a brother living not far. I had a chance to meet him and he did a big favor for me as your will learn later on. Oh, I forgot to tell you the name of the Italian family, their surname was Pedretti. I bought milk from him also, actually most of the time.

As our first winter was closing in on us, I spent a great deal of time in the woods chopping trees down and hauling them close to the house as best as I could. There was an old wagon on the place so I would pile the wood in it and pull it like a horse, many times I would swear and stomp around because it would get too heavy. I remember I didn't want to take some of the wood off because it meant a second trip, even though I had to make several trips I was still bull headed. Winters were mean there, sometimes the snow would pile up greatly and we would not see anyone for two or three days even the mailman wasn't able to come, we would be completely isolated. Looking back at those times I remember it as fun, I remember one time the temperature dipped down to forty below, everything froze, we had no phone, snow piled up everywhere and there we sat next to the kitchen stove, keeping it going day and night. Your mother's father and her brother, I can't remember if it was Uncle Joe or Uncle Charlie, anyway they came out in all that terrible weather thinking for sure we were all frozen solid. They were really worried. When they arrived I was chopping wood in the woods, the difference between the cold in New York and Pennsylvania was and I'm sure still is, Pennsylvania was a dry cold where New York was a damp cold, which is always colder. They sure were relieved to find us well and surviving. They didn't

stay long for fear of getting snowed in, and I went back to chopping wood. In the wintertime we only occupied the kitchen, and the small dining room we used for our bedroom with Rose's crib in there too. We had to use a pee pot for our toilet needs; it was too cold to go in the hall at night, afraid of catching a cold. We kept warm if the stove did not go out during the night. I had it loaded with wood, but sometimes I thought I put in enough but didn't, or the wood was a bit too dry and it would burn too fast, then boy was it cold in the morning. The pee in the pee pot would freeze and I would have to chop it out. Being that we came there in the fall we had not time for a garden so we had to put up with a little hardship the first winter, although papa would always bring a little food to us.

It was in January when I receive a call to work on a government job, me and a few other men. The job was about ten miles from home and since I didn't have a car, I asked Jim Tucker if he would take me with him and I would pay him for his trouble. Well believe me that was the worst job I ever had in my life, it was working in an open field with the cold wind blowing all day long. It was no picnic I can tell you. In those days, I had no thermal underwear so I doubled everything I had on to keep from freezing. I was glad for the job no matter how cold it was; it gave us a little money, and we wanted to be able to save some of it. The job lasted about three months. I remember those cold mornings riding to work; the car would be sputtering while it was getting warmed up. Jim would say, 'Well darn it, cough it up and let's get going.' It was like that every morning all winter. That being our first year there as spring and summer was moving in I noticed along the road, in front of our property ran a fence made out of white Birch also a small summerhouse at the end of the fence. Both fence and summerhouse were falling apart because white Birch doesn't last long, so that spring I went in the woods and cut down more Birch and re-built both fence and summer house. I knew the folks would be going to have a lot of company and they were going to open the summerhouse for vacationing people that worked at the cigar factory. I also planted a little garden for our canning in preparation for the coming of next winter. When summer arrived there were quite a few people staying for a week at a time and some just for weekends. Our best man and his family came, he brought his mother also and after staying a week, when he and his wife left for New York they left his mother and the two children there. I don't know why but Papa asked us to see that whatever she needed to try to get it for her, even money. We told him that we only had fourteen dollars saved. He said if she needed it, we were to give it to her and John would pay us back. Happily there was enough food left to feed her and the children along with us but sadly she borrowed the fourteen dollars. Well we never saw the money, even when we told Papa she had borrowed it. It was not that we wanted to be mean and seem hungry for the small amount of money but it took us almost a year to save it, and that money was saved toward the purchase of a cow, because your mother was carrying Sonny and to have a cow would mean, milk, butter, and cheese for the family and what a help that would be especially in the winter. We felt bad about not getting the money back because a cow was further away without it. I must say we did not enjoy the summers much with all the guests there; it was a great deal of extra work for mom and me. There was always so much to do, cooking, wash dishes, clean rooms, we were servants really, We were never paid for running the house, just lived there free of charge, so what little money I earned outside of the home we needed to save for what we needed that was very important to us. So, it hurt not to be given back the fourteen dollars. Well enough of that.

Mom and I so enjoyed the beautiful country, the stillness of it, even the slight smell of manure spread on the fields in spring, perhaps because we knew it was the end of winter. As a matter of fact, Mr. Pedretti gave me a job one-spring spreading manure for him, I was paid twenty-five cents an hour, that was all saved toward the cow. About that time I got to know a good man by the name of Amos Johnson, I don't recall how we met; he was a stonemason, building homes for whoever hired him. He was a Godsend to us. That man was the finest friend a man could have. He was a big man, strong, heavy built, hard worker. His father in his younger day, they say, could pick up a railroad track and turn it end for end, he was still alive when I knew Amos but he had trouble with his back, I suppose he wore it out lifting heavy things. Amos was married and had two children, they lived in a town nearby, the name of the town was Reeders, and it wasn't far from where we lived. We visited his home a couple times that I remember. He had a funny idea about how he liked his cakes. When his wife was baking a cake in the oven he would stump on the floor to make the cake slump down, his wife would get so angry at him, but that was the way he liked his cake and that's all there was to it. He always gave me work whenever he had anything to build, I would mix the cement, hand him the stones or bricks when he was up on scaffolding. I remember one time he saved me from getting put off the job because I was not a long time resident of Pennsylvania. It was when Jim Tucker's mother's nephew bought some land near her home and decided to build a house, Amos got the contract to build it and after we were working on it for a couple weeks remarks were made to him that I should be let go, not because I didn't work well but because I was not one of them. Well Amos would have none of that and he told them so, thanks to him I kept on working. He knew our condition and he tried to help in any way he could. I remember it was getting close to fall of the year, and we were able to get a pig and sometimes there was no money to purchase corn to feed it, Amos knew my home situation, with Rose and Sonny on the way, this one time he asked me to meet him in the evening, which I did. He had a friend of his with him, he took us to a field of corn that was owned by a well to do farmer in town, and we took a bushel of corn each from the stocks that were cut and stacked together in the field. I did the same thing one night at Mr. Butz's field of corn, and I was almost caught. After I had filled the bag, keep in mind it was getting dark. I put the bag over my shoulder and climbed over the fence, jumping down I saw about fifty to seventy-five feet in front of me a man walking, I thought it was papa so I hurried to catch up and when I did it wasn't papa but Mr. Butz. Well I remember my mind was turning fast, I was asking myself what do I say? Finally I blurted out that I bought a bushel of potatoes and I did not want my father in law to know about it, and asked him not to say anything, and at the same time in my head I was thinking, what would happened if when I was climbing over the fence I found him standing there, what the hell could I say then. Although I am pretty sure he knew what was going on, he never said anything and I never took anymore of his corn. I guess he knew my situation too. At that time corn was fifty cents a bushel, but when you don't have the fifty cents and a family to feed, what else can you do? You can't let a little pig go hungry can you? Not when the pig is a future meal for the family. All I could think at the time was we had to get the pig fattened up for our winter meat. As it was, we only had meat once a week. After a while our sisters and brother who received much more on relief than we did would send us meat now and then and boy would we lick our chops, see city folks received more in relief than country folks, I guess because the folks who were farmers for a long time grew most of their vegetables and raised cattle and pigs. Anyway, we sure appreciated what the family sent us by way of papa. Of course, it wasn't that bad all year, in the summertime when there were visitors in the house we ate pretty well, but we were working for it too. Well anyway, Amos being the good man that he was and with the work he gave me we were able to save enough money to try and buy a cow. We asked Mr. Pedretti and he did have one cow that he would sell, it was a Holstein, a three teat cow he told me she lost a teat when she was small trying to jump over a fence. He wanted eighteen dollars for her, and we did have that much so one-day in the afternoon I went to get her. But after sitting and drinking a few glasses of Apple Cider with Mr. Pedretti, by the way he made the best apple cider I ever tasted, even papa said it was like champ ale. Oh,

getting back to the cow, like I said drinking the apple cider it was dark before I started for home, the distance was about a fourth mile and it was pitch-dark. I don't know if the cow could see I only knew that it was going to be a rough walk home. I had the cow on a short rope walking behind me. I remember as I walked the road if I felt grass under my feet I would move back onto the road. Believe me it was very slow going but the cow and I did make it home; I led her to the barn for the night and headed for the house. That cow was the best cow I ever had it gave us about 20 quarts of milk a day, it was my pet and every day when I came home from work she would be waiting at the fence and follow along the fence up to the barn. I would take care of her the best way I knew how. When we bought her, she was carrying a calf and we anticipated her coming fresh in the later part of the summer. One time when I was at work the pig got loose and your mother, with a big stomach had to try and run her back home. You can imagine trying to catch a pig or even trying to run her back to the pen in your mothers' condition, she really tried but we had to do it when I arrived home from work. We also bought a brooder because we intended to raise some chickens in the winter. About that same time we heard John our best man committed suicide by shooting himself with a shotgun, the reason was he borrowed two-hundred thousand to start a wine factory in an old warehouse during prohibition. The deal fell through, I guess he didn't have a choice, either he did it or the mob would, so he chose his own way. We were very sad, he was a dear friend, but that is the way things were in those days of the depression and prohibition.

All that summer long we had lots of papa's friends staying at the house so there was always plenty of work to do around the place, but the only company that came were adults no small children and we really wanted some little ones to come because Rose was alone and had no one to play with, it was hard for her to learn how to talk. We tried by always saying something to her but it was slow, there is nothing like children learning from other children. Well maybe next year we would always say, young ones may come and visit. I remember one terrible day we were getting ready to wash the floor. I had the water on the stove getting hot, after the water was ready I poured some of the hot water into a pan that was on the floor, Rose was playing with the little dog we had, and I guess she did not see me pour the water, anyway she started to back up and the dog was in front she fell back and hit the pan with the back of her legs and fell in a sitting position. Well she stared to scream, we both turned around realizing what had happen, I lost control of myself, with my hands holding my head I started to pray in polish saying Mother of God! Your mother was right there she pulled Rose out and right away she poured oil over her body, and got someone to take us to the doctor. The doctor complimented mom for keeping her head and doing what shc did. By the time we arrive at the doctor's office Rose had blisters as big as my fist, poor Rosie she must have suffered. The doctor did what he could; he gave us some medicine and home we went. She was sick for quite a while. We had no money at that time and we wanted to give her some better food then what we were eating. I would go out and shoot robins for her, I guess to her it was like a small chicken and she enjoyed eating them. I often think of that dreadful time and thank God that it did not leave her in any way handicapped.

Winter was coming on so we moved to the small dining room for the winter. We set up our brooder stove and we were waiting for the little chicks to hatch. We set the stove in one corner of the same room that we slept in. We wanted to watch them very close and did not want to lose nay a one. I would get up at night and see that everything was in good shape. One night after the chicks had hatched out but were very small the darn stove almost went out, and the chicks got a little cold and some of them got into where the ashes go, not realizing this had happened I closed the door and shook the ashes out to make room for more coal. Yes, you guessed it those poor little chicks suffocated; I found this out the next morning. Thank God we didn't lose but a few. In time, the chicks were too big for the brooder and too small to go outside, we tried to keep them penned up on newspaper but that was a real job. I'll tell you a funny sight to see was when someone sneezed or hollered all the chicks would run for the nearest corner, it sounded like a swoosh then all their necks would stretch and look at you with a question, like "Look what the hell is going on?" That happened very often as you can imagine until I penned them up with chicken wire in the corner.

To supply food for the cow, I got to know a neighbor that had a house built nearby. His name was Mr. Highland, he was an editor for a magazine in New York, and he was married with two little daughters. They would come up for weekends during the summer and his wife and daughters would spend the summers there. I did quite a bit of work for him in their house. The house was all stone outside and all heavy beams inside. I did all the staining of the beams, also other work that needed doing. His wife was a small woman a good looker, she was a blond. But there were many times that they would fight, some Monday mornings when I would go there to work she would have a black eye or black and blue spots on her body. I felt sorry for her because I think he was playing around when in New York and she knew it. The two little girls were nice kids and they had to go through that about every week. I remember while he was there she had a white bathing suit on and in front of him she would come up to me and say how do I look Stanley? It did take me by surprise, I would look at him then at her and say you look very nice, I know she wanted to make him jealous or something but I was very careful around her. On the whole, they were the nicest people that lived close by. Why? Because they were from New York like me not like the Pennsylvania Dutch who lived all around, they were not friendly people to outsiders. Well I have gotten ahead of myself again; I was trying to tell you about the food for the cow. I asked Mr. Highland if I could cut the grass from his fields for my cow, he said I could. When I knew the weather was going to be nice for a few days I would go there with my scythe and cut the grass, let it dry for a few days then with the horse wagon we had in the barn I would pull it to the Highland home, load up the grass and haul it back to our barn. I collected quite a great amount for that winter.

I remember being ready to face the cold days of winter, I remember with the morning chores done I would hurry to get back into the warm kitchen, I remember looking out the window and thinking it seemed just a short while ago the trees were full of leaves, everything was green and full of life, now looking as far as the eye could see there was nothing but naked branches, fields all brown, nature took away the beauty of everything for the winter, it is like saying you better prepare, for the worst is yet to come. Sure enough, one morning you'd get up and look out and see snow everywhere and it was beautiful, the trees take on a different look. Every little section was postcard picture perfect never to be duplicated. After admiring it awhile, you come to your senses and remembered there was much work to be done. You had a bite of breakfast and went to milk the cow, feed the pig, get some wood for the stove, then get the snow shovel and shovel the snow off the porch, make a path to the barn, to the pig pen, then after all that was done you had to go into the woods to chop a tree down for fire wood. Therefore, you grab the ax and start out into the wood looking for the tree that isn't too big, one that will not be too much of a load to carry back to the house. Finding that tree, you stand firm and take a swing and sink the ax, what was that noise? Who else is chopping? You wait quietly to hear if he will strike again but no noise, than you realize it was you, no one else, just the echo in the woods. Then as the tree falls, you hear the cracking and the thud when the tree hits the ground, the sound somewhat muffled by the snow. Yet, the sound is still loud because the snow has a thin layer of ice covering on top and the sound bounces off the snow, as it doesn't absorb all of it. It was so beautiful in the woods, so quiet. I remember how much I enjoyed the beauty as I cut and stacked the wood until I felt I had enough to last a day or two. Then I would sit on a stump for a rest and gaze at the wood, thinking how to get it all to the house where the saw is setup. I couldn't carry it one piece at a time it would take too long and I didn't have a truck, I couldn't ask Mr. Butz to haul it because I didn't have money to pay him. So, I used the wagon that was in the barn, the one I used to gather the grass and hay I gathered for the cow. I remember the first time I cut wood I thought, 'Can I pull a wagon full of wood?' Well what else could I do, so I walked back to get the wagon, pulled it to the wood, loaded it up and after another small rest I tried to pull it like a horse... didn't work, wouldn't budge. I turned around and tried to pull it that way, all that happen is it budged and I fell on my behind, I cursed a little, looked up to the sky but didn't say a word because I knew that God knew what I was thinking, I wanted help. The only solution was to take a little off and make two, maybe three trips, but that was not what I wanted to do. I tried again and finally had to take some wood off; I had to make two trips to get the wood down to the house. After another rest I started up the engine, for the saw, put the belt on the engine pulley and over to the saw table. Now I put a section of the tree on the table and moved it towards the saw blade, which was about twenty-six inches in diameter. It was a good saw, came with the house. After cutting all the wood, I would pile it under the porch to keep it dry. By the time I finished it was near time to milk the cow again, feed the pig, and that was the way the days went by. I remember living in the country, and enjoying all the work. It was our life and we worked hard to support ourselves and our little family, we were happy in the country no matter how hard it got. I am sure you remember your mother saying those years were the happiest time in her life, well we were young and in love.

We spent the winter months mostly indoors, on a nice day we would go out and see the tracks in the snow of birds, rabbits and other animals, I would follow the tracks sometimes just to see where they would lead me but you really never get to the end of the trails as they cress-cross one another so finally you give up. Sometimes I would go rabbit hunting but it took me quite a while to learn how to shoot at a target so I missed plenty of times. I did trap a few woodchucks, really they are ground hogs but they made good eating at the time. The only thing about them was their mouth was like a rats, and sometimes you did not eat them with much gusto, but it was meat. Amos would take me out hunting deer; we did that in the dark with a bright light. We would go slowly on the country road and flash the light across the field and if any deer were there, the light would blind them for a while and that would give us time to shoot one down. One night a state trooper spotted us and Amos had to throw the gun out of the car to the side of the road. We did get stopped and the officer looked for a gun, luckily, we had thrown it out. We went back for the gun after a while and found it. Another night we were lucky and did get ourselves a deer but it did not fall where we shot him and we couldn't find him until the next morning. I have to say deer meat is very delicious; your mother enjoyed it too. Then it came time to butcher our pig and since I had never killed a pig, I asked Mr. Butz to do the task and he obliged. This was the first time I was to watch a pig being killed, Mr. Butz came over with a 22 rifle, and when the pig was looking straight at him he shot it just a little above the eyes, which put the pig down instantly. Then he cut the pig under the chin a little toward the front legs to make all the blood flow out. The knife had to go into the heart to do the job right. Beforehand we had water boiling and, we poured all the water in a large caldron and scald the pig as soon as the bleeding stopped to get all the grime off and the hair we shaved off after the pig was clean. Then Mr. Butz cut the pig down the middle on the belly side and all the innards were taken out. We kept what was edible and buried the rest. Out of the head and feet we made what is called head cheese and boy we had plenty of bacon for a while and big hams that we put in brine, the brine was made out of water and lots of salt and left to soak for a few days then taken out and smoked. I made a smoke house with corrugated roofing sheets and it worked great. The wood I used was Hickory, Sassafras and apple. We bought some lean beef from Mr. Butz and your mom made sausage and we smoked it with the hams. The sausage I can still remember the taste, it was the best I ever tasted, would love to have some now. I can tell you that winter eating was not bad, not bad at all.

During this time, the chickens were getting bigger and looking for a place to roost when their stomachs were full. They would try to jump up on the two-foot chicken wire I had put around to keep them from running all around the room. Some would make it to the top of the wire than fall into the room and we would have to chase them to get them back where they belonged. We couldn't wait until spring to put them into the chicken shed. I had cleaned it out and white washed the entire inside, the only thing wrong with the shed was that it was built too close to a hill and when it rained the water ran right thru it along the floor. I worked on deflecting the water but it didn't do a great deal to correct the problem and we didn't have the money to build a new shed. Now with chickens and a cow we were doing pretty well, we had eggs, milk and plenty of butter. We had an old butter churner, and after we let the milk stand one day we shimmed off the cream and when we had enough we would make butter. I drank quite a bit of buttermilk and once in a while we made ice cream. Mom also made a lot of cheese, which we used for grating and also in sandwiches or just ate, it was delicious, the only thing was if we kept it a too long it would get too hard to eat or grate for that matter and some went to waste. Mr. Pedretti told mom how to make the cheese but he didn't tell her how to keep it soft. I don't know why, because he made lots of it and somehow his stayed soft because he would take a load of it to New York and sell it to stores. Maybe he was afraid we would do the same, people are funny about certain things

About that time, we heard from the city that papa; your mother's father had a little stroke, which was sad especially for your mother. In the spring, he came to the country to stay with us to get his strength back. Mom took care of him and cooked special foods the doctor suggested. The doctor's name was Dr. Diaz. When summer came the doctor and his family would come and stay a week or two, even his in-laws would come with him. Your uncle Charlie, you mom's brother would come up too and take the Doctor hunting for small game. The Doctor sure enjoyed hunting and it got so he would come up very often with your uncle Charlie just to go hunting. Papa was not getting any better and by that time, our chickens were getting nice and big, and papa was to have chicken in his diet, so about every other day we would kill one of the hens. Now here you may think I was not very nice but please keep in mind that this was the first time we were getting somewhere with keeping chickens etc., toward providing ourselves winter food. So after a few days when I saw our chickens were getting fewer I said to your mother that we cannot keep killing off the hens, if we do we will have none left for the winter and perhaps no money even to buy eggs. Come spring we will have to start all over again with chicks if we could afford to buy any, and then go through having to raise them in the house again. Chicks in the house were in no way pleasant. I knew it was hard for her to say anything but her mother was working and I thought she should be seeing to it that papa had what he needed in his diet, at least the chicken. Your mother was reluctant at first to say anything but after a few days she realized something had to be done, so she mentioned it to papa. I don't remember what he said but things were not the same after that. Finally, we all had words and it came to them telling us we were to move out and papa returned to town with grandma. Your mother felt very bad but that was that. I started to sell the things I had accumulated, I sold the chickens, and sadly the little calf that our cow had early in the spring. By the way your mom was the first to spot the little calf out in the field, we carried it to the barn with the mamma following. It was a cute calf and had a mark on its forehead just like its mother, we were going to raise

it to be our second cow, but sadly that never came about. The very hardest thing for me was to sell the cow; I was so attached to it selling it made me feel so bad inside; I think that was the sorriest feeling I can remember of that time. After the fellow I sold her to came with a truck and was driving down the road, we, mom and I were standing on the porch with a sad feeling as the truck pulled away, about three hundred feet away the cow turned around and looked back at us, I think she would miss us too. Do you know I often think about that incident and remark to myself what a nice cow she was. I must tell you this about her, during the early summer, we went to visit my folks in Jersey and I asked Mr. Pedretti to milk the cow a few days as no one was going to be at the house for those few days. He came and she wouldn't let him milk her, so he said and I think he kicked her because when I got home she had a big lump on her lower belly on the milking side; it was as big as a small watermelon. I sure was mad at him but what can you do, nothing. Some farmer told me what to do, I had to pick a certain kind of weed and boil it and then mix it with lard and apply it to the lump, and that did the trick, in a short while the lump was gone. Don't remember what the weed was. Some people say cows are dumb, no sir, that cow knew how well I treated her and she appreciated it. She was the biggest loss to mom and me. After selling everything of ours, we moved to Jamaica over a delicatessen. We didn't stay there long, one night we discovered a little bug on the sheet, a bed bug, well we tore the bed apart, cleaned everything that we thought had to be cleaned, thinking we were rid of them, a week or so later same thing again. Well this time we really went at it. On the floor was a carpet but the carpet was a little long for the room, so we decided to move it around to have it fit better. I turned the carpet back and there they were, a velvet covering of bugs. They must have had a convention and they came from as far as California, a little joke here. Seeing this I quickly took the bed apart leaned it against the wall, rolled the carpet up and threw it out the window. We finished out the month and moved to Brooklyn on Greenwood Ave. Inez lived there with Harold and Josie and Fred lived around the corner. The rent was eighteen dollars a month. Oh, I forgot to tell you, we were on relief. At that time the only extra money any of us, men that is, could make was when the city of New York would get snow, then the street department would put an ad in the paper that anyone on relief could get a job for a few days shoveling snow from the street into the sewer. The sewer was where the manholes were, the city would lift the manhole covers and we would push the snow with those wide shovels into the opening, but let me tell you it was no fun, the temperature was maybe eight or ten above freezing and with the wind blowing believe me you earned your money. About two weeks later, I received a letter telling me to report to work on W.P.A. the work was at a dumpsite. The wages were fifty-two a month. Now let me explain to you what the dumpsite was like. It was a great open space, with two or three large incinerators. The garbage trucks come from all over the area to dump their trash, some of it was dumped in the incinerators to be burned up and then the burned trash is dumped and we were to spread it over the area. There was so much trash brought there that it all couldn't be burned, so some of it was dumped in a large gully. Now I will tell you something about the workings of the W.P.A. It was created by President Roosevelt to keep people working and doing something instead of just collecting money on relief. However, as you know it is politics, and to get a good job it depended again on whom you knew. To proceed with what I have to say, let me explain, there were two groups of us, working under two different foremen. I was put in the group to stay in the open and keep working; the other group was about a thousand feet further on down the field. Their boss (foreman) had more pull with the higher ups so they built themselves a big shanty with whatever they found in the trash, something like tin roofing, large cardboard boxes, stuff like that and in the middle they had a fifty gallon drum in which they burned what they found burnable to keep themselves warm. They also had boxes to sit on when they were tired, and that is how they spent their days and collected their paid. As for us we were not allowed to go where they were, we had to stay outside whether we had work to do or not, we had to stay in the open while waiting for the trucks to bring another load. To keep warm we spent the time looking through the trash that couldn't be burned. That was the time I would find all sorts of things, toasters, flat irons, things like that, I would take them home, fix them and give them to anyone who needed whatever it was. Almost every day I returned home with a box full. Your mother would look forward to the evening when I would return so she could look through the box, like a surprise. That's how it was in those days; I bet you really didn't realize what things were like when you were babies. I never found any money but some fellows did. I really enjoyed finding things, working on them to make them work again. Surprisingly some of the things had nothing wrong with them, I guess the owner wanted a newer model, there were still some people with money to waste at that time, I guess. On the job I made friends with a few nice men, one was a bit odd, we worked together a lot, his enjoyment was to start up a conversation with a few men lead it to a pro and con discussion and when it got to a point of getting heated he would just walk away nice and easy and let the rest fight it out with words. I never did understand what he got out of that.

Many a day we did nothing but lean on the shovels, or whatever tool we had for that day. It was hard especially on those really cold days, but as I think of it now I rather enjoyed it, times were rough for everyone, and we helped each other when we could. I remember one day a girl came to where we were working; she was looking for something to eat. When I say a girl I don't mean a young girl, she was in her early twenties, nationality, Puerto Rican, anyway a fellow who worked with us, he was in his forties took her to his home and then returned to work. He never spoke about her nor did anyone ask him about her as far as I know, I hope he had a wife and they fed and helped her.

She was a nice looking young woman so who knows what his motive was.

Another thing about those hard times was the Communist party was very active, every day they would come by the job and try to enroll whoever they could; the joining fee was ten cents. They would never come out and say that you were joining the communist party they called it something else. I was lucky I never joined or got mixed up with them, those who did I am sure were very sorry later on in life, because the government knew everyone that had joined and it hurt them in many ways through life I am sure. While I worked for the W.P.A. we, your mother and I, were able to save fifteen dollars every month because we intended to go back to the country somewhere. The only furniture we had at the time was the bedroom set we were given by Papa when we were married, we had bought a breakfast set at the Salvation Army store, and Rose had her own crib. We would buy our clothing from the Goodwill or the Salvation Army. Things like work pants, shirts and sometime clothing for Rose.

Many people were doing the same thing those days; there was no way we could afford to shop at a regular store. I was still wearing the suit I was married in and mom had some clothes from when she was single, believe me, we took good care of what we had. The everyday things we either found or bought at the Goodwill.

As I mentioned earlier we were living in the same boarding house as your Aunt Inez and her husband Harold, matter of fact they lived across the hall from us. Papa and mama would come to visit Inez and after a few visits they finally came across to visit us and we became friendly again. We lived there through the winter, me working on the dumpsite, mom taking care of Rose and the house, and we were able to continue to save fifteen dollars a month.

When spring came around we somehow got word of an old couple who needed a man and wife to take care of their place, it was in Delaware Water Gap, that's where the Delaware River separates Pennsylvania from New Jersey. We decided to take the job, mom was to clean the house and I was to take care of the outside things. About two weeks before we were to take the job Rose came down with Whooping cough. I think we asked the lady if it was all right to come anyway. She did not mind and Rose was getting better. We had our own little house to live in, and it was in the country with lots of land and trees, no close neighbors. It was hard there mostly for mom because little Rose would stand by the door and cough and we had to leave her alone, mom couldn't take her to the main house and I couldn't take her outside with me, although it wasn't cold we did not want to take a chance. It was heart breaking to see her standing there red faced, tears in her eyes and coughing. Mom would sneak over to check on her every once in a while. I don't remember how long we were there, I do know that it wasn't very long because being on talking terms with mom's folks again, and I can't say exactly how it came about but papa asked if we would like to go to the big house again. At the time we knew there was another couple there, papa knew the girl when he

156

hired them, so we talked about the couple, we wanted to know what was going to happen to them. The answer was that they were not going to stay long, so we said yes we would like it very much, although your mom and I had a different idea of what we were going to do there this time. After settling in the big house we planted a garden, canned a lot of vegetables, I picked elder berries and made wine. I also made beer and root beer for mom. That fall we picked a lot of apples and brought them to the press mill and made cider. If I remember correctly, it took eighteen bushels to make a fifty-two gallon barrel which we made into apple cider and boy was it good. We canned about everything that we could, grape jelly, elderberry jelly and boy that elderberry jelly was the best jelly I ever tasted. I even made dandelion wine, boy that was some strong wine. The beer was what I liked making best, sometimes while bottling it I would get high, you see you have a rubber hose that you sucked on to get the beer to flow into the bottles and I did more sucking then was needed, it tasted so good. Mom would get mad at me sometimes. Nevertheless, I never got drunk.

Your mother was in a family way at that time with your brother, Sonny and she was putting on a little weight and I remember I used to tease her about it. All in all things were going pretty good at that time. I was getting work with Amos Johnson again; the in-laws of Dr. Diaz bought a corner lot and decided to build a house. I suggested Amos, remember I wrote that he was a stone mason, anyway they hired him and he did the stone work and I did all the carpenter work, that was the first house I ever built, and it was almost two inches out of square, but no one was aware of it but me. While working with Amos, your mom and I saved as much money as we could and decided to buy a piece of land. We got in touch with a Mr. Dyson that was a brother to the first Mr. Dyson that I mentioned earlier and we bought one acre for fifty dollars, we paid for it on time payments. I think that was the biggest thrill we had in our young lives and every chance we got we walked on the acre deciding where to build the house. The lot was on the main road next to papa's land, matter of fact it was on the road that was traveled by more people than the road that papa's house was on. During the summer while staying at the big house, we were relieved of what had been bothering us for a long time. The fact of Rose was not talking like she should have been for her age. That summer Inez's son Charles and Josie's daughter Vicky came and stayed with us for a good spell and to our surprise Rosy picked it up fast, boy that was a relief, she just needed other children around. I remember her calling macaroni, runky.

Winter was going by slowly and we were eating so much better than the last winter, although we only had one animal now, a pig. We had made a few friends by now but never very close ones just some folks to see once in a while. I can't recall why this was so, but there was always something there that we never became close to any of the people living close, maybe because we were from New York and not farmers. One thing I do know and think about at times is that I made a lot of wine and whenever someone dropped by they always wanted a glass or two, and maybe because our being alone so much of the time we felt it was nice to have company even if it was just for a drink or two. I remember this one time when I opened a bottle of the wine it tasted a little like vinegar, so I gave it away freely I would even at times give a whole bottle away, and the more I was free with the wine the more company we had. Then one day I opened another bottle and it tasted good so I opened another and that one was good too, well I stopped giving it away and yes, you guessed it the company stopped coming, but we remained on friendly terms with all of them.

As spring came around again we were anxious to start building our little home, here is the story of how we did just that. By the way, it was the house you were born in Jeannie. Well back to the building of our little house. In the city of Reeders where Amos lived, there was an old icehouse very near a very big lake. You see before refrigerators, in the wintertime lake ice was stored and sold by the block for use in ice boxes which were at that time made of wood, you probably seen one or a picture of one. Anyway, as refrigerators came into being, less and less people depended on ice so this particular icehouse was on its way out. Let me tell you a little bit about the ice and icehouse. In the winter when the lake top would freeze to about fifteen or sixteen inches a team of horses were used to pull a saw over to the lake and they would cut the ice into big sections, then the men would cut it into smaller easy to handle sections. The ice was then put on a conveyor which took it to the icehouse, where it was laid out in a layer that covered the floor then a layer of sawdust would be put on top and then another layer of ice and as each layer was added the conveyor was raised and that is how it went until the building was filled with the ice. From what I remember the building was about four stories high, the walls were about twelve inches thick and packed with sawdust to keep the building cool and that was where we and others who didn't have a refrigerator bought our

ice. Well as I said icehouses were coming to an end and this one was being torn down, so I bought some of the lumber and had it brought to a sawmill and cut to the size I needed for the mansion we were about to build. After we had the lumber, on our land Amos gave me, the name of a carpenter he knew and we hired him to build the first two rooms for us. The size on the outside was twelve by twenty feet we painted it white with red trim because the roof was red. It set back from the road about forty feet, we didn't want any dust coming to the house in the summer from the road that was just dirt. We asked Papa if we could have the old outhouse that was near the big house, after thinking about it for a day or so he said yes and we moved it to serve as our chicken house. I took the thrones out and there was plenty of room for the hens. Your mother was in a family way with sonny, I think I mentioned that earlier, well anyway her father wasn't getting any better and after spending some time in the country at the big house he and your grandma left for the city, he kissed me goodbye and that was the last time we saw him alive, also that was the first time he ever kissed me.

That winter the big house stood empty, I would go see if everything was all right. Do you know that I forgot to tell you the name of that big house, it was named MOUNTAIN REST FARM GUEST HOUSE, there, and now you know.

I wonder why I did such a thing, forgetting to tell you earlier, I guess not thinking right. The following summer your grandmother would stay there all by herself, oh, we kept her company as much as possible, your mother would go to the big house almost every day and many times grandma would come and stay with us. It was a very short distance from our little house to grandma's big house, just a short walk. At times grandma would have friends from the cigar factory come and spend some time with her, one of them was Mr. Genovese, you probably remember him, he was after grandma for a long time even while grandpa was alive. Well anyway, your brother was born at that time, Jan 19th 1937 and we needed more room in that little house of ours so I bought more lumber and built the add-on myself, it was twelve by twenty-four with a little room for our bathroom. We also bought three more acres, now we had four acres and the whole field was ours, in one corner there were a few pine trees about eight or ten feet tall, we were really happy about that because there weren't many pine trees at all in that area. I built a pigpen and also we put in a large garden, everything you can name we planted, I even planted buckwheat and I cradled it myself. In the summer the family of mom's would come and there was plenty to eat, we would build a fire and put the corn in with the husks on and they cooked that way, it was delicious. We enjoyed it very much because we enjoyed company and we were hungry for someone to talk with and see. Although we had this little house all built there were things missing, we had no water and no electricity. The water we got by having three forty quart cans, I would put them on the wagon and go down the road near Mr. Butz place and by the road there was a spring, I would fill the cans and pull the wagon home. For light, we had a Coleman lamp, which gave plenty of light for the kitchen and part of the dining room. Do you know I forgot to mention that Sonny was born by then, he was born in the big house and let me mention that as he began to walk he was very bow legged, but as the months went by he out grew it. Another thing I must tell you is Rose was always eating ashes out to the stove on the sneak, or she would eat the ashes out of any ash tray she would get her hands on. Your mother tried everything to break her of it, she even put bitter stuff in her mouth to see if that would work but it didn't. Yes I have to say we were dumb in a sense, instead of going to a doctor to find out what was causing this we let the poor kid go through this craving for some kind of mineral in the ashes, although she stopped on her own before too long. Later on we found out she needed calcium; I hope after reading this she forgives us.

At this time in my story Sonny was growing up and Rose had company to play with. One entire summer your Aunt Josie and Uncle Fred left their daughter Violet with us. Rose and Sonny were very glad to have her there and we were too as it kept Sonny and Rose from under foot. We never asked anyone for one penny when anyone was with us, we were only too glad to have their company. That year Fred brought us a refrigerator in appreciation for our keeping Violet all summer. Oh, yes you might ask, I thought you didn't have any electricity, well let me put it straight, when we build the first two rooms we didn't as I said we used the Coleman lamp, in fact we bought another Coleman, but when we built the add-on the electric company came by and installed the juice, so we were really thankful for the refrigerator. Now that the electric was there, we had to get a well drilled. I went to the same man Mr. Dyson and asked him for a three hundred dollar loan, he didn't ask me to sign any papers against the property, it was just a piece of paper torn out of a writing pad saying I owed him three hundred dollars, I guess he knew I was good for it seeing how I paid back the money I owed on the four acres I bought from him. After I was sure of the money I cut a branch from an apple tree in the formation of a Y, I put the two twigs leading from the single twig, one in each hand closing my hand and putting my thumbs on the ends of the twig, and putting a little pressure against the ends. Now by putting the branch in front of me about chest high the single end in front I began to walk, first I tried the side on the left of our house and sure enough the front of the twig was being pulled down by itself. That was a sign water was where the twig was pointing, but then I realized that my septic tank will be on that side, I can't drill for water there, so I went to the right side and began again with the twig and when it was being pulled down it was right by the porch which was better for me and closer to the house, wrong or right, I decided to get the well drillers and proceed. They started to drill where I had chosen and they went down forty feet, sixty feet... I remember I started to worry a bit, what if there was no water, then seventy-feet, it cost a dollar fifty a foot to drill, gee I had over one hundred dollars in it now and no water, down eighty feet, now I really began to worry, but at eighty-five feet they hit water. They told me I could get four and one half gallons per minute, well that was plenty good for our family actually more than we could use. After they tapped it I dug a square ditch around it and put a concrete wall on each side with a cement floor, I bought a deep well pump and set it in the hole, made a square cover for it and we had water pumped into the house, but not into the bathroom, we flushed the bowl by another means, you know how. Boy having our own water saved me a lot of work, I didn't have to haul water from the spring anymore, and I pulled the wagon to the big barn and left it there. Summer was about over and we had all our canning complete. That year I even planted Buckwheat as I wrote earlier. I don't know for what reason I just wanted to have something to grow that I could cradle as I cut it, although the buckwheat did not go to waste because I fed it to the chickens.

Now I will write about winter coming on and all that needed doing in preparation, I wonder if you have ever taken notice that there are two periods in the year that a person goes through a different change, one of the times is in the late fall, especially if you live in the country, you go through the act of preparing for the cold days. Cutting wood to keep you and your family warm, gathering the food you planted and finding a good storage place to keep it until the time you will need it. You know that you will spend more time in-doors, even when you work elsewhere because when you arrive home, you will stay in-doors. It's a small form of hibernation. Do you think I am right? It is like closing yourself from the outside world in a small way. The other time of change is in the spring, this time of year you seem to open the doors wide to the world, you lift up the shades on the windows to let in the light, you step outside to the smell of the earth and the smell of the barn manure being spread on the fields. You want to listen to the birds, to see the leaves coming forth on the branches, to look up in the sky and holler aloud...I am glad to be here and thank you God for letting me

enjoy all your creation, everything looks so wonderful, life is beginning anew.

Well back to where I was in my story. Winter is upon us; I was called to report for work, in Tannersville about a mile from our house. I walk to work each day, you see in Tannersville there is a creek and the federal government was giving the town funds to build up the banks along the creek with stone so the banks wouldn't wash away any further in the big rains. This is where I found out how a human being can be unthinking and unkind to another human being who is just trying to get along in hard times for himself and his family. I always prided myself as a good worker, no matter for whom I worked or where I worked, but to get on with my story. There was an election going on in Tannersville, this crumb was running for the towns supervisor, on a platform to cut expenses. Well he won the election and became the overseer to this job of reinforcing the creek walls, the job I was on. Unluckily I developed a terrible cold but instead of staying home, I went to work, and believe me I was sick, fever and all. I was doing my job sliding stones to Amos then at the end of that day this crumb gave me a pink slip, Fired! Now this job was a federal project, paid for by the government to make work for the needy instead of paying relief, you were put to work which is better than sitting home, that's how it used to be, not like it is today with people sitting around and collecting money each month, well anyway every time I think of it I can't get it through my head how a man can think so small, he fired me because I was not from the same state as the rest of them, I was from New York. At that time, the people of Pennsylvania were that way; at least many were that I came in contact with. The state may be beautiful but the people spoiled it at that time.

While living in our little house in the winter we would buy a detective paperback tear it in two and sit near the warm stove each reading our half, when we finished we would exchange and start reading again. Rose and Sonny had tricycles and they would ride around the four rooms in a circle until it was time for bed. Your mom was in a family way again, this time with you, Jeannie. Oh, about how that job turned out, I had to go to the relief office and tell them what happened, but like the rest of Pennsylvania, they punished me for a few weeks and then put me on relief. I finally spelled that word right, relief not relieve, but you probably fixed it by now.

I don't remember if grandma lived in the big house all winter or not but anyway with Mr. Genovese seeing grandma quite often the two of them decided to open the big house once again as a summer place for any of their friends to come, and pay of course. You might ask, was Mr. Genovese married, yes he was all the time while he was seeing grandma, you see his wife was in a mental institute. He would visit his wife every week but soon after he and grandma were seeing each other his wife passed away, so he and grandma became closer as time went by. Well I am not writing about them so I will end about them here.

As it became spring again, 1938 because it was the year you, Jeannie were born. By the way you were the only one born in our little house. Back to my story, it was spring again and everything was coming to life, I got my garden ready for planting, I still did a little work for Mr. Highland and some work for Amos, as I said way early in this part of my story Amos was a Godsend to us. As spring started we gave a little help to grandma and Mr. Genovese to get the big house in order for the summer, but like the other summer when Papa was alive the boarding house was never a good money making deal. When you realize that you had to feed the people three meals a day, make their beds and serve them all for between fifteen and twenty dollars a week it just didn't pay. They found that out so the idea to run it anytime in the future was dead.

About this time you were born, I can't tell you just when, I am very poor on remembering birthdays, I leave that to your mother. I just looked in mom's book and now I can say, you were born September sixth nineteen-thirty-eight, I guess you know that. As I mentioned earlier you were born in our little house, and mom had a rough time giving birth to you. In those days the doctors did nothing to help a woman in any way, he had a board under her with two handles one for each hand, the handles were hooked to the board by chain, well she busted the two handles right off the board. Poor mom she really had a rough time. Then after you were born we had troubles with you, no matter what kind of milk we gave you it didn't agree with your system. The doctor prescribed different things and nothing helped, we were getting very worried about your weight loss, but finally someone suggested we try condensed milk, well that worked fine and our little family grew from then on.

On the upper part of our four acres near the Pine trees, a large part of it was wild strawberries, I would go and pick them and mom would make an eighteen-inch pie, if you never tasted wild strawberries, you are missing something delicious. The only thing with wild strawberries is it takes so long to pick a pot full, it's like picking blueberries.

I should have mentioned this before, the time that I am writing about now we had a car, a 1930 ford convertible with a rumble seat, so any time we wanted to go shopping we went in style, we traveled to the city of Stroudsburg about eighteen miles from home. The tires on the car were not very good and I remember going to Stroudsburg and by the time we arrived home, we had about four flat tires. I recall another time while I was fixing a flat something drew my attention away and I didn't turn the bolts tight enough so while we were going up a hill the car went one way and the wheel the other, after that every time I applied the brakes it made a thumping sound I guess I dented the brake drum. I should say I had put the wheel back on, the way I've written it, it sounds like I drove without the wheel. Well, I learned to be more careful when fixing a tire. I do hope you are able to understand this story the way I have been writing it, I know I keep jumping from one thing to another, but

while sitting here and trying to remember all the past, it's like a big wheel in my mind, that keeps going around and as these things come to mind I write them, I know it would be impossible for me to put them all down completely as they happen. I am sure it could be done but for me it would take much too long.

Now I must get back to grandma, a little after grandpa died she realized the running of the boarding house was not going to pay so the time had come to think about how to keep the monthly payments going, she did not want to just walk away from it, she wanted to salvage some money for herself so she put the farm on the market to sell but times were rough and there were no buyers. Somehow, she came up with the idea to put it up for auction. However, before she did your mother and I asked her if she would give us a plot of land right in the back of our property. We figured we should get something for all the help we had given her and grandpa from the time they bought the place. The answer was yes and we were happy because that plot of land was three and half acres all of woods that I could cut firewood and also our complete property would be worth that much more. After her farm sold, she bought a house in East Stroudsburg twenty-one miles from us. On weekends, we would go down and visit with her. All though Mr. Genovese was there quite often to keep her company, I can't remember how long she lived there but she sold that house and moved to the city and went back to working at the cigar factory.

Now to get back to our lives, for the next couple years it was just the usual routine, work when I could make a little money and living off the land as much as we could. As the years went by rumors of war began to be more frequent, things didn't look good at all. At this time my sister Rose came over to visit and I asked her if she was aware of any work in the factories around New Jersey, and through her I found a job in Harrison New Jersey and this was just about the time the war broke out. I don't know if I should call that a lucky break for me or not but getting a job at this factory saved me from having to go to war, because in Pennsylvania the army was taking everybody children or not, besides I was not registered there so I was not called. While working in Harrison your mother was still living in the country, I would go home on weekends. I remember mom saying that with me not there; when the thunderstorms would come she would hang blankets over the window so the lighting would not come in. I guess she and you children became frightened. Here again I am getting way ahead of my story. The reason is this, up until now I have been typing with one finger, then all of a sudden I said to myself, "Listen dum-dum you are doing all this typing with one finger why don't you try using two fingers, with all the typing you have been doing you could have learned to type with two fingers by now."

Oh, while thinking this, I over taxed my brain and ran off track again. Ah, well let's get back to my story. Hope you can piece this whole story together.

Back to before I found the job my sister told me about, I was still at home in our little house. I found work in a boarding house about a half a mile away. It was called Brouckhousen, a German place. It was the busiest place around, all Germans lived there, let me dwell into this a little more so you will know why it was so busy. Long before the war the Germans all over the United States had their own clubs and societies, they called themselves the Bund, something like the K.K.K. or the Communist party. They were conspiring against our government. The average citizen did not know it at the time. These people worked for Hitler they even had their own army in this country. By this, I mean they were teaching all their teens how to handle a gun and all things pertaining to working against this country. Of course, I didn't know this either at the time. There were weekends when our relatives came over we would go to one of their restaurants nearby for a glass of beer or a little dancing. Anyway when I was offered a job at the Brouckhousen, I was offered thirty dollars a month which was very little but I was only doing odd jobs, things like painting, plumbing or any little thing that might need doing so I said what the heck, I will take it and see what comes of it. The first day I reported for work and put in my eight hours and went home, the next day I reported for work and the lady asked me where I was in the evening, I said I went home after I put in eight hours. Oh, she said, you can't do that you have to stay here until we tell you, you can go home. Well I thought about it, thirty dollars a month, that's bad enough for eight hours a day however as I said I was willing to do that as the work wasn't hard but if I had to put in more hours I would be earning maybe less than ten cents an hour, the answer I came up with was, I would rather lay down and starve to death then work for those kind of wages, so I quit. About a year later, the husband caught the wife making love with the cook and he killed them both and then killed himself, and their boy inherited the boarding house. Getting back to the Bunds, when the war broke out the government arrested all of them and put them in a camp. I don't imagine you can recall

Major Bowes Amateur Hour; he also was a Nazi Spy. He was sending signals to Germany by playing certain songs on his show. Anyway that was what I heard then. Now that I finished telling this little ditty, I will go back to where I left off, back to where I was working in New Jersey. Since I had a steady job, we decided to move to the city once more, we felt it would be better for us in the long run. With our bigger family and my working steady life would be better in the city, so the city it was. While I was working, we saved enough money to rent an apartment near my sister Rose and her husband. At first, I lived with them and went home for weekends like I said earlier. I then asked Rose and George her husband if your mother and you kids could come and stay while we looked for an apartment, they said okay, that turned out to be a big mistake. All though she was my sister, I must say the truth. If I remember correctly we lived there two weeks, and I remember how upset your mother was, the reason being my sister, having always been a domineering person, and her children could do no wrong and her kids knew they could get away with anything they abused little Sonny in any way they could. If he had a toy that he was playing with they would take it away and tease him, they would receive no reprimand from my sister. Mom would tell me this and it made me angry but we had to suffer, or I should say Sonny suffer. The day came when we found a place to live and one weekend George, Rose's husband helped move us from Pennsylvania. I must say that George was a very nice man, not because he helped us but he just was a good man, my sister did not appreciate him, and they parted company some years later. He went to work in Texas for the same company that he worked for in New Jersey, which was the Otis Elevator Company. One time he must have been in California and he called our house on Euclid St, he was to come and visit us but never showed up, the reason, I don't know. When I went back to New Jersey, the last time I returned there, I went to attend the wedding of my sister Betty's daughter, I did see George from a distance, with a lady I believe was his wife, but he never came close enough to say hello, I am sorry I never approach him. I know my sister Rose was always sorry they divorced but you can't turn the clock back, now can you?

Now back again to my story. After moving into the house we rented I noticed some railroad tracks but didn't pay much attention to them, that first night just after we all fell asleep low and behold the darn house started to shake it woke us all, scaring you kids, it felt like an earth-quick, it was a freight train going by. Well we thought, 'that is over and back to sleep we went, but not for long, another train came through from the opposite direction. What could we do? Nothing! We had to stay there one month as we paid the first month's rent and anyway we had to look for another place. We found another place, this one on Temple St in Newark New Jersey, the rent was reasonable, but no hot water, we had to heat our own when we wanted to bathe, however, there were no trains nearby. We stayed there close to a year, lots of colored people living around and this was in the time that Joe Louis was the champ, and every time he'd win a fight there would be fights among the whites and the colored especially with the Italians, so we found another place about four or five blocks away, an apartment that was on the second floor, the owner's name was Mr. Martino. I may be wrong but I think I remember he had three daughters. This was a six family house, the owners also owned an Italian grocery store, we became quite good friends with them, and a couple times we went on a picnic with the family. All the girls liked your mom very much and often would ask her advice on things. We lived there for quite a long time, but like every place no matter how good it might be it always had its drawbacks and this place was no exception. Like I said six families lived there, over us lived a family with two boys and they were bastards to put it bluntly, they, like my sisters kids could do no wrong as far as their mother was concerned. The thing that upset us was in the summer time when we would open the window and want to look outside by putting our head out, those boys, if they

170

were at their window the same time you were at your window they would spit on your head. We would tell the owners but to no avail, they did nothing. I can understand the position they were in, not wanting to lose a tenant, but I must admit your mother and I were hurt by their lack of concern because we were friends after all, money was more important to them I guess.

However luck was with us because we received a letter from Pennsylvania, someone was interested in purchasing our home and property. We sent them a letter stating the price we would like to have, while waiting for a reply life went on as usual. Let me tell you a little about the kind of work I did in the factory, it was a wire factory, Driver Harris Co. it may still be there. My position was in the acid room, the friend that helped me get this job worked in the same room. The area of the room was about twenty-five feet by thirty-five feet, and on one side of the room was a big air vent to take up the acid fumes, this air vent worked like a chimney and along the same wall were four tubs about twenty inches high and about three feet in diameter, the rest of the wall was taken up with tubs made out of brick with wood on the outside of the brick. The wire that was drawn into the size that was wanted was taken to a place where it was enameled, by that I mean it was put in a salt bath that was heated to such a temperature that the salt was melted and remained in a liquid form, the wire was left in this bath for a specific amount of time, then it was brought out and put into a water bath to cool, the wire was red hot, when it went into the cold water it made a terrific noise throughout the factory. When cooled it was brought to our area to clean. The outer shell of dirt was very hard that is the reason for the acid. The acid procedure was like so, in the tub we put ten gallons of Muriatic acid; one pitcher of nitric acid then filled the tub with water to about six inches from the top. Then we put a rubber hose in the liquid, turned on the steam and the mixture would get hot with the wire in it. We would watch it carefully and every so often, we would pull the wire out and put the micrometer on it to see that the acid would not take it down too far. The work itself was not bad, it was the acid that was not pleasant to work with, we had to wear boots all the time, a rubber apron and cotton gloves, the threads of your pants and shirt seems would rot and soon you were wearing flared pants and open sleeves shirts. My bosses name was Mr. Murray, he was a heavy smoker, always coughing; he had worked there a very long time and lived in Morristown New Jersey. After a time I was transferred to the next room. I was coating flat nickel bands used to make wristwatch bands to give them a copper color. I did this by using water with Sulphuric acid with blue stone and steel chips. The steel chips came from the Crucible Steel Mills that was about two blocks from the factory I worked in. That mill was owned by a New England company and they produced cannons and all other armaments for this country during the Second World War. If I had stayed at Driver Harris I would have become the supervisor of that department Mr. Murray was giving me more and more of the layout work and I in turn gave it to the other men. I really didn't want to be there that long, I wondered about the chemicals and perhaps that was the reason Mr. Murray coughed so much. Anyway, I worked there a good spell but I always kept my ears open for a transfer. While working there the friend who got me the job became sick and it was not long and he passed away of cancer of the lungs, he was a very heavy smoker too, I am sure the acid fumes didn't do him any good. The family sued the company for not having the acid room in good working order, yes; they came and asked me a lot of questions. I could do no more then tell them the truth, and the truth was it was killing to work there and to be a smoker at the same time well who knows what the combination does to the body. Next to the room I worked in was the lime room. In the lime room, there were two big vats about six feet wide and five feet deep, sunken in the ground; there was a fence around the vats to prevent anyone falling in, with a gate on one end that swung open when needed. The vats were always kept hot with the steam pipes that were within the tubs. In the vats was lime, which was used to coat the wire and to enable it to go through the die more easily. After the wire was dipped in the lime, it was put on hand trucks and pushed into the drying room, then after about three or four hours it was pushed into the next room where the wire was drawn. Now to explain a little about the procedure of drawing the wire, here goes! The machine used to do this process was about twelve feet long and on the machine were four round columns about eighteen inches across and twenty inches high. The wire was put on a turntable, which was on the floor; the worker would take one end of the wire and put it between two rollers, which made the end of the wire come to a point. In the front of each round column was a box about six by six inch, made of heavy steel, in the front of the box there was a hole and a die made of very hard steel was put in back of that hole inside the box but pushed up against that hole. The box was filled with soap powder, then the wire was shoved through that die until it stuck out of the box, a clamp was put on the end of the wire and hooked to the round column then the machine was started. The wire being pulled through that smaller hole in the die made the wire smaller. The same procedure was followed through in each four boxes that made the wire smaller and smaller until the wire reaches the size wanted. Sometimes if it needed to be even smaller it would then have to go back to the enameling room, back through the acid room and the same thing all over again with the columns and boxes. I hope you understand, as I would hate to start all over again with my explanation. Oh, by the way a man did fall in the lime vat and went to meet his maker, all though it was before my time there.

As I mentioned earlier, I kept my ears open for a nicer job in another department and one did come along, it was in the enameling room on the third floor, not the enameling room I just told you about. I asked for the position and got it. This was the kind of position one dreams about, you could work with your Sunday best on and not get dirty. I forgot to say this plant was working twenty-four hours a day, every day, because of the furnaces having to be always burning. It would take too long to get them hot enough if they were shut down through the nights. How our working hours worked was as follows, the shifts were 8 am to 4 pm, 4 pm to midnight, midnight to 8 am, every two weeks we would change shifts. The midnight to 8 am was the hardest because from 3 am to 6 am it was hard to keep your eyes open, for me anyway.

The new work I was doing will be hard to explain, but here goes. The furnaces were between twenty to twenty-five feet long, in it were about twenty-five 3/8 inch pipes sticking out one end about six inches, on the other end they stuck out about six feet and were resting in a square tank filled with water. The furnace was heated to maybe eighteen hundred degrees. Now going back to the back of the machine we would take a roll of wire and put it on a turn spindle, take the loose end of the wire and push it through one of those pipes that was in the furnace until it came out the other end, now keep in mind that this wire was hard, by hard I mean it was springy and by going through the furnace it became red hot and at the same time became soft and that was what was needed. Next, we would take the end of the wire that we just pushed through and wind it on a spool that was on a machine just ahead. The spools were geared to move slowly giving the wire time to get soft as it moved through the furnace and water. Now if the spools were big and you set your machine with twenty such spools you had nothing to do for maybe the rest of the night but watch that all went well, also I should say the finer the wire the longer it takes to spool it up, which is what I mean when I said it was a dream of a job.

When the war broke out, I was classified 4F because I was married with children and working in a defense factory. The factory was C.I.O., we were paid a salary plus a bonus for the amount of work we turned out, that was good and also bad, it is a long story and if you are interested ask me next time we are together and I will tell you all about it.

About this time, we received a letter in answer to our letter offering to sell our little home. I think I told you we asked for a certain amount and we received an offer for $1,450.00, we talked it over and decided we wouldn't be going back to live there so we accepted the offer. I left my Ford and many other things there and never went back to see how things were. I have often thought about going back, just to see the place again, who knows maybe someday we will. Now what to do with the money, sure we wanted to buy a house but anything in that line was new to us, however as they say, if you don't look you don't see, or is it nothing ventured, nothing gained? Well anyway, take your pick they mean about the same thing. Time came to start looking, we didn't want to keep paying rent, and common sense tells you that if you own your own home the money you pay in rent could be buying a home and building equity which is like a savings. It's like killing two stones with one bird... did you catch that? So the first chance we had we went to a real estate office and saw the house in Nutley, New Jersey, and liked it. The price was right, $3,500.00, so we bought it. Now don't forget this was still in hard times, ninety percent of the homes on the market at that time were owned by the banks. You might ask why? I'll tell you, because people could not pay the mortgage payments even when they were low. The banks had so many homes that they would ask people to just pay the interest on the mortgage until they were able start paying on the note. It was really rough for so many. Well that said, it didn't take us long to move in. The house itself had three rooms upstairs with a bath and down stairs was the kitchen, dining room, living room and a nice sun parlor as we called it in those days. It was a room with lots of windows and lots of sun in the summertime. The house was on a dead-end street and we liked that for you kids, you were able to play in the street and not worry about traffic. It also was walking distance to the shopping center, the bus to Newark was just a block away and that was good for me, although we did have a car it was better to take the bus in the winter. That is if you could get on. Going to work was all right but coming home was bad because all the buses were full so you had to walk in the direction of where the bus was going and after several people got off you had a chance to get on. It was very bad when a big snowfall came because then you most likely would have to walk home all the way. However, as I look back I would do it all over again if I could only get to that age again. Yes I know those doors are closed for good now. After getting settled in we bought a dog, we named him Blacky do you remember Jeannie? (Yes I do, I remember when dad brought the pup home he called us kids into the kitchen and he sounded angry, I must have been five of six years old. He said, 'Now just look at that trash bag who spilled it over?' We looked and there was Blacky.)

In a short time, I bought a piece of land next to our house from the city. It was a small piece, about fifteen feet wide and the length of our land going back. I filled it in to make it level with our land and built a barbeque and in front, I built a stone fence about two feet high. You and Sonny used to stand on it in the hot summer rainstorms. All of you went to St. Mary's Catholic School a very short distance from the house and every Sunday we all went to church. On the way, home we would stop at the bakery on Market Street and buy some coffee cakes for breakfast. Do you remember walking to the movies on Bloomfield Blvd., on many Saturday afternoons? Sometimes you all went to the one on Franklin Ave in the city of Nutley. I remember the time Rose decided to leave home, I guess she had an argument with mom and she told mom that when she got bigger she would leave, mom probably said, why don't you leave now, so Rose took her up on it. I guess mom's words came faster then she wanted and she couldn't retract them, so Rose got dressed, mom put her up a lunch for the trip as a starter and Rose was on her way. I was working outside and I would turn around once in a while to see what Rose was doing. As she walked up the block, I would see her look back now and then to see if anyone was going to come after her. I think she wanted that so much, I felt sorry but she had to learn. But a wonderful thing happen on her way after turning the corner she found an old tire and knowing that I save all kinds of things she came back bringing the tire to me. I think somehow she realized that we would miss her and she decided to stay with her family and we were glad to have her stay. Do you remember Jeannie when you didn't return from school and it was getting dark, you were about seven years old, you had gone off with a friend after school. Mom and I were scared to death but thank God you arrive home.

That house didn't have a garage so I built one out of cement blocks, I said before that the street was a dead end, it really was not because beyond the house down the street was a wide open field and in Nutley there was a factory making Naulgahide and the company would dump its remnants and some gooey thick stuff in a big ditch. Every so often a fire would break out and the fire department would have to come and try to put it out, but it seemed that no sooner than they left the fire would start up again. It seemed like it was always burning underground. Of course, that was before any environmentalists were around. Yes, in those days, the big corporations did dirty this world for us, but it will get cleaned up soon, I hope.

I remember the nice Christmases we had on Bayard Street, oh I forgot to write the address in Nutley, it was 21 Bayard Street, I know you remember that but I don't know if Rose or Sonny remembers it. Anyway, we had some really nice Christmases. Mom and I would dress the tree after you all went to bed and we would put all the presents under the tree. In the morning, we would wake you all up and send you all down stairs without us, to be surprised. Then when all the noise would stop we would go down and join in the unwrapping of the presents. Oh, I know we had some nice Christmases in California too, but in Nutley, you were all younger and that made it more enjoyable and sweeter to remember. I am not going to try and bring up all the things that you should know because I want you to try and remember some of it yourself, just sit back and shut your eyes and think back. Even though you were the youngest, you still can remember some of it I am sure. Sit back, shut your eyes and think back, I am sure you will enjoy your childhood, parts of it anyway. Do you remember going to the frozen little lake by the church and skating on two runner skates that clipped to you shoes like roller skates? Oh, to relive it once more and to be able to put more emphasis on enjoying the family not the world outside. I wonder if you remember the day the war ended, everyone on the block ran outside yelling, crying, hugging each other that was a wonderful day.

I think we lived there on Bayard Street a little over five years, while living there we went to visit my folks about every week in our Plymouth. Do you remember going out with the Cappolo's who lived across the street from us and getting wet from the rain storm: do you remember your Grandma living with us and Mr. Genovese coming to stay over the weekends. Then they moved to Jersey City and were working in the cigar factory nearby. After a while Mr. Genovese passed away. From then on Grandma was with Inez a lot until she too passed on, which was much later, when you were married and in a family way yourself with Florence.

Now comes the part of why we moved to California. As you know, I had been to California in my younger days and I had always wanted to go back and live there, but never got down to doing it. One day Uncle Charlie and Aunt Carrie came by loaded with their belonging and they were headed for California, well that did it for me, the house went up for sale, it took about three months to sell and we were on our way. Now I am sure you all remember everything from there on, am I right? Now for me to just say "The End", doesn't seem right, I feel like there should be more to it than just saying, this is the end. Should I say I do hope you enjoyed my story, not because of the writing because I am not a good writer, and I know Jeannie, you will have a lot of work ahead of you if you choose to do

something with these memories and I feel
you will because as I said before you like
to write. I think I just wanted to leave you
a bit of my history and yours too. I wrote
this from the stand point of bringing back
a little memory of happy times that you
might have enjoyed in your younger days
and maybe had forgotten or not thought
of in a long time. Or were they your happy
days? Could they have been made
happier by someone and they were not? If
so and if it is through our fault please
forgive us, I know we made mistakes in
one way or another but maybe those
mistakes could not be avoided and maybe
I am wrong for trying to apologize I leave
that to your judgment. I will end here by
really saying this is the end of my story of
our earlier years together.

My father was seventy-eight when he, with one finger, then with two fingers as you read in his story, typed his early life as best he could. I tried to not change or add to his story; however I found it necessary to change much of the format, refine some of the writing, correct spelling, grammar and punctuation to the best of my ability in order to make his story flow well and be easier to read.

This is his remarkable story. It has taken me several years to complete this project and I am happy to have done so because that is what he wanted me to do. For me personally, it has been a joy to my heart and soul, and at times, I have felt he was here with me in spirit. I hope you have found the story to your liking, I felt the need to share his story because of the simplicity and the beauty of an America many of us have never known. In the problems of today's world it may be right to visit and appreciate the hard times and the courage of an earlier time. Might I add that if you have a family story of your own or a loved one write it as a gift to your family, my father's notes were a most wonderful gift to me and my children, his grandchildren.

Many of the cities, small towns, streets, and areas which my father mentions can be found on the Internet when searched by its name, address, date, (early 1900's) or searched by image.

Thank you,

About Jean Caroline

Jean Caroline was born Jean Caroline Priscilla, where she was born the story tells, the family moved to Santa Monica, California in 1947 when she was eight years old and there she grew up. In 1973 her husband, herself and their four children moved to the country, an acreage just outside the town of Florence, Oregon. She now resides in the city of Florence, Oregon.

Jean has written three previous books, although not published as yet. Her next book to be published will be a children's chapter book titled, **Billy McBride and the Silver Spurs.**

8335819R10110

Printed in Great Britain
by Amazon.co.uk, Ltd.,
Marston Gate.